Portrait of Rye

Portrait of Rye

With some sketches of places
worth visiting within easy reach of the
Ancient Town

Malcolm Saville

Illustrated by John C. Allsup

Published by Mark O'Hanlon

First published 1976
Second edition 1999

ISBN 0 9528059 2 8

British Library Cataloguing in Publication Data.
A catalogue record for this book is available from the British Library.

Printed in Great Britain by Rea Valley Printers, Shrewsbury.

Published by

Mark O'Hanlon

10 Bilford Road, Worcester WR3 8QA

To the Memory of my
Grandfather

Reverend Alfred Thomas Saville

Missionary in the South Seas and
Minister of Rye Congregational Church
1878 – 1905

Acknowledgements

With gratitude I acknowledge help and encouragement from the Reverend Doctor Alec Vidler of Rye; the Reverend Canon John Williams, Vicar of Rye; Mr Geoffrey Bagley, Honorary Curator of Rye Museum and author of the Official Guide to Rye. Miss Anne Roper, M.B.E., historian of Romney Marsh and Mr Kenneth Clark, enthusiastic Ryer and historian, who has checked my facts with tact and patience. My thanks also to the authors - many no longer with us - of the books mentioned in the Bibliography, who have kept alive my interest in, and love for, this precious corner of England where I was born, and to which I have now come home again.

And last, but certainly not least, I salute... my friend, the poet, Patric Dickinson, for embellishing my efforts.

M.S. 1976
Chelsea Cottage
Winchelsea

[Reprinted from the 1976 edition of *Portrait of Rye*]

Malcolm Saville died on 30 June 1982. His ashes are buried in the Garden of Remembrance at the Church of St. Thomas, Winchelsea.

Thank you to everyone who has given support to bringing this book back into print. In particular, thanks to the Estate of the late Malcolm Saville, Lesley Hadcroft, Guy Hawley, Frank Palmer, Michael Saville and Louise Stothard.

The manuscript has been updated and edited by Mark O'Hanlon after consultation with Guy Hawley, Frank Palmer and Michael Saville, so that it is relevant for publication in the late 1990s but remains as close as possible to the original. Where a particular passage has been identified as being out of date the text has been amended to reflect an accurate picture of today. Where this has not been possible, or in instances where this would lose large sections of the text, it has been annotated to show that it was accurate in 1976 - *[Ed. 1976]*. In places, the text has also been annotated with the editor's comments recorded in brackets - *[Ed.]*. *Rye*, a poem by Patric Dickinson, is reproduced by kind permission © Sheila Dickinson.

M.O'H 1999

Contents

Acknowledgements   6

Sketch Map of Rye   8

Chapter:

1   Rye Town   9

2   The Story of Vanished Men   15

3   Around the Town   45

4   Round and About   89

RYE   A poem by Patric Dickinson   117

Bibliography   118

Appendix   119

Index   124

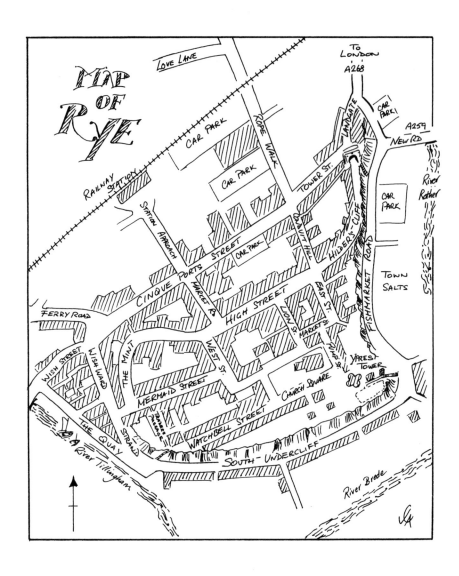

MAP OF RYE

8

Chapter One:

Rye Town

This book might be described as the consummation of a long love affair. I cannot remember when I first came to Rye, and have lost count of how many times I have returned. Now that I live in her sister 'Ancient Towne' of Winchelsea *[Ed. 1971-81]* it is as if I have never left this corner of Sussex where history has been fashioned and which means so much to those who have discovered it.

Wherever my travels have taken me in Britain, or across the Channel which has now deserted these once famous ports, I know now that Rye is the town by which I tend to judge all others. And the one to which I have always wanted to return.

My sense of wonder for this 'port of stranded pride' has never waned. I have seen it in peace and war and in all seasons. To me, as to hundreds of thousands of visitors from all parts of the world, Rye is unforgettable. Some say it has charm. Perhaps, but it is not just this dubious quality which brings people of all ages and from so many different countries back to it. With dismay, I have sometimes heard it described as quaint, and occasionally as 'so foreign', as if this was important.

As we shall see, Rye - and Winchelsea too - have had considerable experience of the French down the centuries and have usually returned measure for measure. Our town, in particular, gave refuge to hundreds of Huguenots in the sixteenth and seventeenth century but I believe Rye is remembered, so often with nostalgia, because she is typically English. You will find no great houses of the aristocracy in her narrow streets because she was a town of merchants, sailors, boat builders, fishermen - and often of smugglers and pirates.

Rye is today a town of three rivers. A port deserted by the sea but now a living, busy, thriving market town with still a few fishing boats which come up the Rother's muddy tide and unload within two hundred yards of its ancient walls. And Rye still preserves her cobbled streets along which our visitors trudge with clicking cameras and stand patiently in Lion Street to watch, and hear, the Quarter Boys of the famous clock of the biggest parish church in Sussex, strike their bells.

Rye is not typically Sussex in appearance but with her sister ports on the Kentish coast to her east, and Winchelsea and Hastings to the west, we state proudly that she represents the South Country. Her enemies - if we forget the occasional but reprehensible, piracy of the fleets of Rye and Winchelsea in our own waters - have always been the foreign foes of England and her monarchs. Much evidence of those belligerent years still remains. The Royal Military Canal, born on Pett Level below Winchelsea, joining the Rother, through the Brede below Rye, becomes a canal again at Iden Lock. Much wider now, this pleasant tree-bordered waterway running across the Romney Marsh to Hythe, reminds us that this was constructed as a defence against Napoleon.

The ruins of Henry VIII's clover-leaf Camber Castle still stand between Rye and Winchelsea. Although the scars of the indiscriminate bombardment of the Second World War are healed now, some ruins of our coast defences can be discovered in surprising places a mile or so inland. Kent and Sussex have not only proved to be British bastions in the past but are still the main gateway to Europe.

Rye's situation is dramatic and unique. There is always a fascination about a town on a hill but Rye's red roofs and grey walls cling to a pyramid of rock which rises abruptly from flat land once covered by the sea. But the rock is not a perfect pyramid because it slopes more gently towards the landward side and the peak is crowned by the squat tower of the great parish church. From all approaches by road - and even from the railway - it is easy to appreciate that Rye was once an island.

It is not surprising that this town is probably the most sketched and painted in Britain. Little wonder that artists find Rye irresistible. Although the streets running east and west are invariably straight, the High Street and its narrow extension known as the Mint, are both intriguingly curved. Few of the houses are alike. Rye's architecture spans the centuries and almost every building is a surprise. Many are above spacious cellars which were undoubtedly used for storing contraband brought by 'ponies trotting in the dark' across the marshes between Dungeness and Pett.

Later we shall explore the streets of Rye. Every inhabitant and every visitor has special memories of its delights. Impressions vary with the time of year and time of day. Rye is like that. A town of moods but I am sure that mid-morning at the height of the tourist season should be avoided. Not even Rye's High Street is spared the giant delivery van.

For me the best time to savour Rye's magic is at dusk in autumn or winter. As daylight fades, the lights begin to glow in the windows of the houses clustered round the church. From the Gungarden we look down on Rock Channel and the brown water of the Rother as the tide slips out to the sea beyond the straggle of houses at Rye Harbour two miles distant. We can still see the line of giant pylons as they stride inland from the Nuclear Power Station on the shadowy horizon but, as we watch, a soft carpet of grey mist creeps across the marsh and seems to lap the sides of the rock on which we stand. Lights are flashing now where the river joins the sea, and miles away across the bay, the new lighthouse at Dungeness signals a warning to shipping in the Channel.

As we turn back to the town the massive bulk of Ypres Tower looms through the dusk on our right. This is one of Rye's oldest buildings. It was raised in the thirteenth century and was first known as the Baddings Tower. After walking a little further over the cobbles of what used to be known as Pump Street - unfortunately now called Church Square - we find ourselves in Market Street between the Town Hall and the Flushing Inn. Rye's delightful shops are closing now. At one time open fires would be lit - or rekindled - in the inns and hotels. Wood was plentiful in these parts and there is no welcome on an autumn night like an open fire.

The medieval town has electric lights and car parks now but it is not too difficult to imagine how the streets looked when lit only by lanterns or flickering torches. We should go down to the High Street by one of three narrow streets which we shall explore later and as we wander about the town we may well be struck by the evocative challenge of the names of so many of the streets and narrow ways. Consider the promise of discovery in daylight, for instance, of Watchbell Street, Mermaid Street, Lion Street, Cinque Ports Street, Trader's Passage, Ferry Road, Conduit Hill, Wish Ward, Wish Street, Fishmarket Road, Landgate, Tower Street, The Mint and Rope Walk.

And although it may be dark by now, stroll down Market Road to the railway station, the yard of which is used as a bus terminus and which will be very busy as the country people who work in Rye make for home. There is nothing precious or 'olde-worlde' about this part of the town. You will hear the slow speech and cheerful banter of those from the villages of the Sussex and Kent borders. Later in the evening, if you have the wish to do so, you may meet some real Ryers in the pubs.

But Rye has something for everybody in all seasons. I mention winter first because it is easier to appreciate the town when the pavements are not so crowded with sightseers. Easier then to realize that this medieval town has seen bloodshed and pillage. As we shall see in the next chapter, Elizabeth I came here and dubbed it with the proud title of 'Rye Royal'. It was customary, on the Saturday nearest November 5th, for Rye to celebrate her own version of Guy Fawkes night with a torchlight procession through her ancient streets culminating in a mighty bonfire on the Town Salts below the East Cliff. The celebration lapsed in 1974 but has been revived again in more recent years. Typically, Rye calls this Rye Fawkes Night. Symbolically an old boat is dragged through the town before a huge bonfire is lit on the Town Salts. The flicker of torches, the roar of the flames and the martial music of the bands seem to belong to the past rather than symbolizing the present, although the young people in costume on their floats in the procession invariably succeed in being topical with a touch of cheerful vulgarity.

Winter often brings snow to the south-east corner of Britain when the wind is from the north but the gales to which we are most used come roaring in from the south-west. When they synchronize - as they often seem to do - with the high tides of autumn, the Rother overspills its banks and Rye Bay is creamed with foam. In the streets we taste salt on our lips and sometimes tiles come tumbling from the ancient roofs.

The gales come with the real spring tides too but then the winter is behind us. These are the nights when the moon is full and to see her shedding her pale radiance across the flat marsh, over Camber Castle and Winchelsea on her wooded hill a little further west, is a rare experience. There are some alive today who remember waiting and watching on such clear nights for the spearhead of Hitler's attacks on this vulnerable stretch of coastline. It was an attack that never came.

We can be certain that Rye is always ready to be looked at and, when spring arrives, with billowing white clouds against a blue sky the colour of the distant sea, you should be there. I once, in another book, described the setting of Rye as "green and white." Not so long ago this was an accurate description because the green of the flat, fertile marsh seen from the Gungarden or the church tower was of a remarkable translucence. There were no cultivated fields to be seen from these viewpoints. Everywhere was green pasture dotted with white sheep. Today there are many cultivated fields, for wheat and rape are grown extensively. However, there must still be thousands of the fine Romney sheep on Walland, Denge and Romney Marshes, growing fat and strong on some of the richest grazing land in the country. And in a few weeks there will be thousands more when the lambs arrive and their plaintive cries come to us on the evening breeze from the sea. Inland, the Sussex countryside is varied and very beautiful. It is well wooded too and thick with anemones, bluebells and primroses in spring.

In summer the town becomes almost cosmopolitan. It is difficult to realize that the very same streets through which so many visitors are strolling have seen war, plague and fire. Time and time again Ryers have stubbornly rebuilt their town from its ashes.

It is difficult to assess the magnetism of this historic little town. I have come to believe that in this unhappy age of standardization and mediocrity, Rye stands alone, sufficient to itself. It is not indifferent to the outside world but history has left its mark. One of the town's historians wrote that "it had an incredible hold upon life and its beloved rock." Life was tough in a Cinque Port in the fierce, early days of their history.

'God Save Englonde and ye Towne of Rye' are the closing words of its old Customal but there is a much later phrase which has become accepted as an apt description of those who were born in Sussex - 'We won't be druv.' Rye is proud to be in Sussex. She has successfully guarded the south-east corner of this delectable county through the ages. Perhaps that is her secret.

Chapter Two:

The Story of Vanished Men

A portrait is not a history book but what men did influences the place where they lived and loved and fought and died. In the following chapters we are going to look at Rye as it is today but before doing so we must learn something of its history since the beginning of the eleventh century.

Rye has been fortunate in having writers who have extolled its virtues - Jeake, Holloway, Vidler and more recently, Geoffrey Bagley, author of one of the admirable Official Guides to the town, and Kenneth Clark author of several specialized publications dealing with the history of the district. Not a word of this chapter could have been written without reference to their investigations and records.

It has been suggested that both Rye and Old Winchelsea once formed part of the Roman city of Staninges but no real evidence for this seems to exist. It is more likely that, as Holloway suggests, the sandstone rock on which Rye now stands was first used by fishermen for net drying; that they first built huts and then houses and later a town. The coastline was vastly different in those days and what we now call Rye must have been an island with no approach except by sea. We do know that King Canute granted the English Manor of Rameslie - an area which contained Rye and Winchelsea - to the Abbey of Fecamp in Normandy some 75 miles away and both towns came under monastic control for more than two centuries.

Whether this influence was good or bad we do not know but there can be no doubt that from this time Rye was in constant communication with France. England had been invaded by the French Dauphin, Louis, in 1216-17 and Rye itself had been occupied. It was only the failure of Louis to take Dover Castle and his defeat at sea by the Ports in 1217 that forced the French to withdraw. Worse still, Normandy had been lost in John's reign, which meant that the Channel was no longer an Anglo-Norman lake. It was in the light of these events that Henry III determined to take ships to defend the vulnerable coasts of south-east England.

So, in 1247 Henry struck a bargain with the monks. Rye and Winchelsea became Crown property while the Abbot of Fecamp received some inland manors instead. The Norman masters departed and the two ancient towns won their independence and became important and busy seaports.

Meanwhile, we are told by the historian Vidler that Rameslie, with its port, was being gradually eaten away by the sea. "Its citizens were taking the wise precaution, the same as that taken later in the town of Winchelsea, to remove their possessions - while retaining their identity, their charters and privileges - to a safer site. They had selected a little fishing village lying behind the old Winchelsea, washed on all sides by the sea at high water and commanding the road to London. It was an ideal spot. Rameslie they could not call it, as Rameslie still partly existed, so they named it La Rie, the old French name for a waste spot, and the same as a town in Normandy in which Fecamp also possessed certain rights."

So Rye was born but it must be remembered that Winchelsea was not yet on its hill and probably in much greater danger on a shingle spit, possibly where Camber Sands are now. Old Winchelsea succumbed to a number of thirteenth century storms; that of 1287 only confirmed a decision already taken to build a new town on the hill.

Rye and Winchelsea were limbs of Hastings until 1190 when, because of their growing importance and excellent fishing fleets, they were admitted into the Confederation of the Cinque Ports,

THE YPRES TOWER FROM THE GUNGARDEN

JOHN ALLEN

comprising at this time: Hastings, Romney, Hythe, Dover and Sandwich. From that time their correct title was the 'Cinque Ports and Two Ancient Towns.' Now, only Dover remains a port for the succession of storms which drowned Winchelsea changed the coastline too, altered the course of the River Rother bringing it to Rye and nearly destroyed Romney as a port.

The early years of the fourteenth century were particularly important to Rye. She was now an incorporated borough electing her own Mayor and under the direct rule of a friendly king. Gone were the days of a foreign overlord and no doubt she assumed the responsibility of guarding the mouth of the joint harbour she shared with Winchelsea, which was still struggling to re-establish her greatness on the hill of Iham two miles away.

Rye took her chances. Her beautiful church now crowned the town and close by the sturdy tower of defence - now known as the Ypres Tower - defied from the southern cliffs those of her enemies who approached from the sea. It is not easy today to imagine what a busy medieval seaport was like but we can be sure that the little cobbled streets we walk today were thronged with pirates, merchants, fishermen, sailors and craftsmen including the skilled boat builders. It must have had watermills and windmills and historians tell us that it was famous for its pottery; a craft which is still practised in the town. It also contributed five ships to the Cinque Ports fleet.

The sea which had brought prosperity was sometimes an enemy, because in the middle of the fourteenth century the eastern part of the town was swept away. Then, only five days after the death of her friend Edward III in 1377, Rye was sacked furiously by the French. This really was a sanguinary business and although soon avenged, the streets ran with blood and the invaders utterly ruined the walled town. Stow's account of the massacre, which in part is quoted in Holloway's history of the town, says: "They, within five hours, brought it wholly into ashes with the church that then was there, of a wonderful beauty, conveying away four of the richest of the towne, and slaying sixty-six, left not above eight in the towne. Forty-two hogsheads of wine they carried thence to their ships, with the rest of their booty, and left the towne desolate."

This vivid account seems incomplete. What were the Ryers doing? Did they not put up a fight? Were they hopelessly surprised and outnumbered? The truth seems to be that this was an occasion when the Ryers did not show much courage. It seems their confidence in the strength of the new walls was misplaced and that the authorities had ordered that nobody should remove his goods from the town, hoping that the inhabitants would be heartened by this act. They were not and, reluctant to leave their possessions, they put up a poor fight. The French stayed for a few days while ravaging the surrounding countryside but were betrayed by one of their own foragers who was captured in one of the nearby villages. He confessed the French plans to the Abbot of Battle who put all his available men into armour and led them into Winchelsea which was put in a state of defence. The French heard this and sailed for home with their booty, leaving Rye a smouldering ruin.

Rallied by their Mayor and the King's Bailiff, both of whom had escaped with their lives, Ryers counted their dead and recovered something of their spirit. First they hanged the spiritless traitors believed responsible for the loss of their town. Then, when they realized to their ultimate shame that the invaders had stolen and sailed away with the bells of their precious church, they swore fearful oaths of vengeance on their hereditary enemies - the hated French.

With renewed courage and vigour they restored the breaches in the town walls. They rebuilt their houses in the following year and then, with the willing help of the men of Winchelsea, took action and sailed for Normandy. History does not record how many men and ships arrived by night off a town called Peter's Haven but the Ryers and their friends landed and gave the French a taste of their own medicine. The church bells were recovered, the town was set on fire and the men returned home well pleased!

And so it went on. The French returned in 1380 and dealt with Winchelsea but by the end of the century Rye was slowly recovering from the disasters of this period of her history. The church had been rebuilt although we are told, "it never recovered its former beauty." Nevertheless, some of the houses that now exist may have been rebuilt at this time.

Prosperity seems to have returned to Rye by the beginning of the sixteenth century when it claimed to have one of the finest of the Cinque Port harbours. Her merchants and traders were doing well. Shops were built on the Strand. Her fishermen were proud of their calling and successful - their catches were often sent to London. The church benefited also from the wills of Rye's wealthy citizens. During the reign of Henry VIII, Camber Castle was built on a spit of shingle which is now a flat marsh beyond the town and Rye harbour. It is one of the 'clover leaf' fortresses built by the king as a defence against the French but it was never attacked. By the end of 1643 Camber Castle had been abandoned and became derelict. It still stands as a lonely sentinel with the sea a mile or more away.

In November 1562 the first Protestant refugees from France and Flanders arrived in Rye - an important date in the history of the town. Rouen and Dieppe had been taken by the Constables of France from the Prince of Conde with whom Queen Elizabeth I, now on the throne, had made a treaty. She also supported the Protestant party with men and munitions. As was the custom of those days, the victors had sacked the two towns with revolting cruelty and Rye's first arrivals, fleeing from the terror, numbered 500. A month later another boat arrived with refuges but some must have returned after a patched up peace.

Six years later there was another influx but the greatest of all followed the massacre of St. Bartholomew on the 24th August 1572.

History tells us, and we should be glad of it, that these poor people were welcomed by the Ryers. During the first half of the century the population of many towns and cities of Britain had been depleted by the plague and we do not know precisely how many refugees returned to France. Historian Vidler recalls that many made their homes in Rye and eventually were absorbed into the local population. At about this time over 1500 people of French extraction were living in the town. The names of some of today's inhabitants and some of the houses bear witness to the peaceful invasion.

In August 1573 Queen Elizabeth I made her only visit to the town. We do not know many details, except that before her arrival she rested in Northiam a few miles to the north-west, where she sat under an oak on the village green and "feasted". She stayed three days in Rye, on one of which she visited Winchelsea and, was so impressed with its buildings and town planning, that she named it 'Little London'.

Presumably this was a compliment but Winchelsea in its new situation, planned and with its early growth supervised by Edward I, was a modern medieval town, while crowded Rye was typical of the period. Anyway, before leaving Rye the Queen was presented with a purse of one hundred gold angels by her loyal subjects and she dubbed the town 'Rye Royal'.

Vidler also recalls that by the following year the French refugees were settling down so well that they had their own church. A safe conduct was also granted to a captain and French crew of nineteen in a ship called the *Hound* to, "sail to Norway and to Rochelle with merchandise." There is a house called La Rochelle today at the top of East Street.

The men and ships of both Rye and Winchelsea must have fought against the Spanish Armada in 1588. We know little about this except that a year later the Queen presented the town "with six brass guns beautifully ornamented with the arms of Spain, which stood on the spot called the Green."

This share of the victorious battle against the Armada is almost the last naval service that the town performed. Rye's income was falling. The harbour was silting up and no longer deep enough to hold the large ships of war which were now necessary for defence and attrition. In fact, after the days of the Armada, Rye became a trading town and was much helped by the Huguenot refugees from France and Flanders.

At the opening of the seventeenth century Elizabeth I was still on the throne. Rye's town walls were still intact except on the east side which was now protected by the river and cliffs but the harbour, on which the town's prosperity had always depended, was a constant anxiety. The sea was retreating and the marshes drained, and life for Ryers began to change.

In the 70th year of her life and the 45th of her glorious reign, Queen Elizabeth died. Nobody seemed to know much about her successor but the Cinque Ports had to send representatives to the coronation under the direction of the Lord Warden. The years slipped by. Charles I did not show much interest in Rye but there were other notabilities who did. Sir Anthony van Dyck, for instance, made four drawings of Rye, which is remarkable considering that he did not specialize in landscapes or buildings. One of these sketches may be seen in the Uffizi Galleries in Florence. Another man whose name is still remembered in the town and, becomes the first of our own 'Vanished Men' to be specially recorded, was Thomas Peacocke. In 1636 he was chosen a Jurat, or magistrate, of the town. In 1638 he made his will and died soon after. This will was particularly important because it supplied a long-standing want - a Free School for the lads of Rye. For this, he granted his house, which is still standing on the north side of the High Street, facing Lion Street. It is a magnificent red brick example of the period's architecture and remained a school until 1907 when a new school was built by the East Sussex County Council on the marshes to the north of the town. Thomas Peacocke's name has since been given to a new Comprehensive School and, after many alarms, we can say today that the facade is all that remains of Peacocke's original Grammar School in the High Street.

Another Ryer whose name must be recorded at this stage of the town's history is Samuel Jeake, born in 1623, son of a prosperous baker and appointed Town Clerk twenty-six years later. Samuel was a remarkable man in many ways. Brought up a Presbyterian, he was also an astrologer who frequently consulted the heavens and there is no doubt that he was also an able lawyer. Later in life he proved to be a painstaking and enthusiastic historian of the Cinque Ports and left many valuable records to which all writers who have followed him owe a debt. There were three Samuel Jeakes - father, son and grandson - and each contributed much to the town. No evidence exists as to where the first Samuel lived but the second, the diarist, who married Elizabeth Hartshorn when she was twelve or thirteen, lived at Hartshorn House (formerly known as the Old Hospital) in Mermaid Street.

Rye did not prosper much under the Commonwealth. The church was in a ruinous state and during this period a strict supervision was instituted over all travellers passing through the town both to and from the Continent. In 1657 two companies of foot soldiers were quartered in Rye and were billeted compulsorily in private houses and inns, which suggests that Cromwell was aware that the decaying port could still play an important part in the defence of the country. The Protector died the following year and the Mayors and Jurats of all the Cinque Port towns were notified at once that "the most noble and illustrious Lord, the Lord Richard, eldest sonne of his said late Highness, to succeede him in the Government of these Nations." With this proclamation came a promise that all men in the service of his late father would continue to hold the same offices under the new Lord Protector.

As we know, this situation did not last very long and in 1661 arrangements were made for the new King's coronation. Sir John Fagge and Marke Thomas the Mayor were appointed to represent the ancient rights of the town and to help carry the canopy over the King.

Early in 1682 more French Protestants began to arrive in Rye following a new wave of persecution by Louis XIV. It is pleasant to record that those fugitives were again warmly welcomed by the inhabitants, many of whom were descended from those who had found succour in the ancient town in the sixteenth century. Vidler recalls that "they were allowed to use the parish church from eight to ten in the morning and from twelve to two in the afternoon with the full approval of the Vicar." The leaden Communion flagon used by them is still in Rye Church.

In October 1685, following the revocation of the Edict of Nantes, a further number followed and many of their descendants still live in the town. We are told that supplies were sent down from time to time - presumably from London by Royal command - to help the people of Rye to care for the distressed refugees. It is worth recording that the refugees were great manufacturers and probably the most enterprising people in Europe at this time. Within a few years of their arrival in England they started new industries wherever they settled and Rye was no exception.

In October 1690 the first Samuel Jeake died in his 67th year. His son Samuel II, who was left everything his father possessed, seems to have been a brilliant young man. Vidler tells us that at the age of 19, "he was somewhat acquainted with Latin, Greek, Hebrew, rhetoric, logic, poetry, natural philosophy, arithmetic, geometry, geography, theology, drawing, heraldry and history." Like his father he was a nonconformist and astrologer - a strange combination of faiths. He built the Jeakes' Storehouse which still

24

stands on the south side of Mermaid Street. On this he placed a horoscope showing the appearance of the heavens on the date that the foundation stone was laid. He was elected a freeman of Rye and died in 1699 at the age of 44 leaving only one son (Samuel, of course) who was only aged two at the time of his father's death. Elected a Jurat in 1720, Samuel III remained unmarried, served the town well and died in 1770, so ending the long association of the Jeake family with Rye.

The names of most of the 'Vanished Men' of Rye's history in the eighteenth century are familiar to us today. At this time the walls of the town, together with the Landgate and the Strandgate at the bottom of Mermaid Street, were in reasonable repair although the state of the church, after years of neglect, was deplorable. There were Quakers in the town now and they bought a Meeting House and burial ground in Mermaid Street. Two houses there today are named 'Quaker House' and 'Elders House'.

Two other family names always remembered in Rye are Grebell and Lamb. Representatives of both served the town several times in the Mayoral chair. Thomas Grebell began his reign in 1699, but was Mayor again in 1705 and 1713. His brother Jeremiah then took turns of office in 1715 and 1718. In 1720, Allen Grebell, son of Thomas, succeeded and chose his brother-in-law James Lamb to be his freeman. The third of the Samuel Jeakes, now 22, also became a Jurat.

Lamb House at the top of West Street is one of Rye's architectural glories and we shall visit it later. It was built by James Lamb in the early 1720s and the family occupied it for over a century. During one of James' early years of Mayoral office Rye was again honoured by a Royal visit but it was not a particularly happy occasion! H. M. King George I was returning from Hanover early in the New Year of 1725 when his ship was driven into Rye Bay by an appalling storm. Vidler records with considerable under-emphasis, "Being alarmed for the King's safety, he was put ashore on the beach... and from there he had to walk all the way to Rye, where he arrived much fatigued."

Under the circumstances this is not surprising! Presumably he was accompanied. Probably he had never heard of Rye and there is little doubt that he could not speak English. It is possible however that both the Royal guest and his host were able to converse in Latin. Anyway, James Lamb was warned of his approaching honour and set out on horseback with some of his Jurats to meet their unexpected visitor. The actual meeting is not recorded but it must have been dramatic - possibly traumatic for both guest and host. Anyway, James Lamb escorted the tubby, irascible and storm-battered German to his own house and gave him his own bedroom. The great gale gave place to snow and communication with London was impossible but it seems George I received a friendly welcome and stayed at Lamb House for four nights. A few days before Mrs Lamb had given birth to a boy and the King at once agreed to stand Godfather. He presented the child with a handsome silver bowl inscribed, "The Gift of His Majesty King George to his Godson George Lambe, Anno Dom 1725." When able to resume his journey Rye gave him a typically loyal send-off with the trained band lining the High Street and the church bells ringing below a ship's flag fluttering bravely in the wind above the tower.

Time and time again the name of Lamb appears in Rye's history books and it is now time to retell the story of the murder (a story which has received much embellishment over the years) which was perpetrated in the churchyard in 1742. Grebells and Lambs had intermarried and at this time James' brother-in-law, Allen Grebell, lived almost opposite Lamb House. On the evening of March 16th there was to be a celebration for James' third son John, who had entered the service of H. M. Customs. The revenue sloop on which he was to serve was lying at the present Fishmarket and was to sail with the tide the following morning. The party was to

WEST STREET

be aboard and James, who had been a widower for five years, was presumably to be the guest of honour. Unfortunately he was far from well that evening and, when Allen Grebell strolled across the street to see him, James asked him to take his place and explain the situation to his son. Grebell agreed but said he must go home first to collect his cloak. There was little time to spare and he was persuaded to borrow James' cloak for the evening. This was the cause of his death.

Some seven years previously James, in the course of his magisterial duties, had fined a butcher named John Breads, for giving short weight. For thirty years James Lamb had been Deputy Controller of Customs in Rye. We shall deal with the smugglers of Rye later but there is no doubt that smuggling was a way of life at this time and those who enforced the law were not likely to be popular with many of the inhabitants. John Breads had a butchery in the yard behind the Flushing Inn and the latter was certainly used by smugglers. There is no evidence that James Lamb was the sort of man who would ever shirk an unpleasant duty and Breads, furious at being fined for what, no doubt, he considered normal business practice, determined to be revenged on the Mayor.

Everyone in Rye knew about the Lambs' celebration but nobody in the town knew that Allen had taken his brother-in-law's place and was wearing his cloak. Towards midnight, Grebell was returning home through the churchyard. No doubt he was in a happy frame of mind but whether he intended to call in at Lamb House we shall never know. The moon was up and the shadows of the tombstones were thick on the ground. Behind one of these the butcher Breads was hiding, armed with a large knife from his slaughter house. As the man he presumed to be James Lamb passed him, he stabbed him twice in the chest. Extraordinary as it seems, Grebell, who was also a widower, did not realize what had happened to him but staggered home and told his manservant that a drunken man had knocked against him in the churchyard and, that as he was feeling shaken, he would rest downstairs for a while. His man retired but that is not the end of the story, for we move on to the supernatural - if indeed a vivid dream in which our loved ones return can be so considered.

On this same night James Lamb was visited three times by his dead wife. On each occasion she begged him to go and see, "if all is well with Allen. I am alarmed about him."

The third time, when day was breaking, James put on some clothes and went across the street to his brother-in-law's house. The sleepy manservant answered his knocking, admitted that his master had come home rather disturbed at midnight and had stayed downstairs. James sent him up to Allen's bedroom to see how he was but the man returned in alarm with the news that he was not there, nor had the bed been used. Together they searched the house and found Allen Grebell sitting in his chair beside the ashes of a dead fire with the fatal, mayoral cloak still around him. He had bled to death, probably unaware of what had happened to him.

The murderer was not difficult to find although the manservant was at first under some suspicion. Breads, who must sadly have under-estimated the powers of law and order, was shouting round the town in a drunken frenzy that, "Butchers should kill Lambs." He was promptly arrested and a blood-stained knife with his initials on the handle was found where he had thrown it away in the churchyard. This careless and seemingly stupid murderer was brought to trial the following May, in a warehouse on the Strand which had been temporarily fitted up as a court hall. The Mayor, James Lamb, presided but because of his own relationship with the murdered man, had summoned a Counsellor-at-Law to help him and a Grand Jury of fourteen. The details of the crime seem rather complicated. The function of a Grand Jury was to decide whether the prisoner should be tried *on the indictment as drawn*. There was also, of course, a petty jury whose duty it was to try him for the crime. Breads was eventually found guilty and when asked if he had anything to say, shouted "I did not mean to kill Mr Grebell, it was you I meant it for and I would murder you now if I could."

So the murderer was sentenced to death and sent to the Ypres Tower. A fortnight later he was hanged just outside the Strand Gate. Next day the body was taken down and encased in chains in a blacksmith's shop in the Mint and then hung up on a gibbet in a field, known to this day as Gibbet Marsh, just outside the town, by the windmill.

It is curious that bloodthirsty criminals are often remembered longer than those who are a credit to the society in which they live. Breads is a typical example and those who are interested may care to know that part of his skull and the chains in which his body was exposed for 50 years, are still stored in the Town Hall. A replica can also be seen in the Heritage Centre on the Strand.

During the second half of the eighteenth century, the wealthy and able family of Lambs dominated the parochial history of Rye. James died in November 1756. He was buried in the parish of St. Andrew, Holborn in London (where he had been born) but his sons, Thomas and James, continued to serve the town.

Although the Reverend John Wesley was certainly not one of Rye's 'Vanished Men', it must be recorded at this time of the town's history, that he first visited Rye in 1758 when he stayed for a few days in October. He came several times in the following years and a note in his diary under 22nd November 1773 records, "found abundance of people willing to hear the good word; at Rye in particular. And they do many things gladly but they will not part with the accursed thing smuggling, so I fear with regard to these, that our labour will be in vain."

And so we come to the stories of the vanished smugglers of Rye but before doing so it is pleasant to report that dear old John Wesley's labour was not in vain. Proof may be seen in the beautiful chapel in Church Square which we shall visit later.

Smuggling seems always to have been regarded as a romantic sort of 'cops and robbers' game in which the often maligned forces of law and order were constantly outwitted by sporting outlaws. But there was nothing much of the Robin Hood attitude about the smugglers of the Kent and Sussex coastline. There were two historical aspects of illegal trading. The first, during the fifteenth, sixteenth and seventeenth centuries, was the export of wool from Romney Marsh sheep. Those who worked this racket were known as 'Owlers'. Later, came the import of spirits (particularly French brandy) lace, silk and tea. Anyway, whether smuggling wool out or brandy and tea in, no part of England was so active throughout the centuries as the coast between Hythe and Hastings. No wonder so many buildings in Rye have secret hiding places for contraband. Nor surprising that sympathy for smuggling was the rule rather than the exception, while those who denounced it were despised. In the mid-eighteenth century we are told that "Intimidation reigned supreme. Magistrates hesitated to arrest lest they should be turned out of house and home. Juries failed to convict on the clearest evidence." And this was because the jury was always packed with smugglers. Mr Kenneth Clark, in his admirable monograph, *Many a Bloody Affray* reminds us that, "the smuggler was a public benefactor in the eyes of the local people or, at most an honest thief - but not a criminal. This attitude, coupled with the low standards of morality persisted until the coming of Free Trade and the establishment of the nonconformist conscience in the nineteenth century."

Informers were ruthlessly murdered, often with unspeakable atrocities. Greed is always ugly. Smuggling was very profitable and many were implicated. Many horses were used in the trade and often were commandeered from the stables of farmers, parsons and squires. It was usual to leave a 'tub' in payment and that usually kept the recipient prudently quiet.

The smugglers of fact were not romantic adventurers but, much more likely, gangs of bloody desperadoes who greatly outnumbered the troops and Preventive Officers sent against them. The most notorious of these was known as the Hawkhurst Gang, of whom many stories have been told. When convenient, these ruffians refreshed themselves in the bar of the Mermaid Inn, where nobody dared to interfere with them. They eventually came to grief in 1747 when they were caught and sentenced to death after their most abominable crime. This story has been told many times and concerns the unspeakable torture and murder of two men, who were betrayed when on their way to Chichester to give information to the Justices against the gang. They were caught before they got there, lashed to the back of one horse, dragged and flogged round the countryside and their faces slashed with knives. One of them was then buried alive upright in a hole and the other hurled head first down a well and stoned to death. There were other obscene tortures.

In a lighter vein was another story of smugglers told by my grandfather in a lecture on 'Ancient Rye' which he gave to the Rye Mutual Improvement Society on 4th January, 1890. I quote: "A story is told that about 100 years ago, a large cargo of contraband spirits was landed early one Sunday morning near Camber. The Custom House officers were on the alert. The smugglers got their possessions as far as Guldeford but, finding it dangerous to proceed further, got, by some means, the church key and deposited safely the goods within the sacred edifice. The clerk then went to the minister and promised him two of the tubs if he would keep silence. In a short time the news was spread about that there would be no service that day, in consequence of the indisposition of the minister. On the Monday evening the cargo was safely conveyed into Rye, except two tubs for the minister and two for the clerk."

But enough of smugglers, although they will never be forgotten in Rye. The years slip by. In 1801 Thomas Lamb, in his 83rd year,

32

was elected Mayor for the twentieth and last time. He still lived in the house his father had occupied at the top of West Street and did not die until 1804. A memorial on the north wall of the church nave records, "in his disposition he was benevolent and humane, in his manners cheerful and social, in the discharge of every relative duty faithful." "Fair enough," we might say today but an opinion not universally shared at the time. Another of Rye's 'Vanished Men' who gave his life to his town.

At the beginning of the nineteenth century, we must remember that Napoleon, the self-styled Emperor of France, was massing troops at Bologne for the invasion of England. Once again, Rye volunteers were called up for duty but the British fleet held command of the Channel and, on 21st October 1805, Nelson finally crushed the French fleet at Trafalgar. England was saved again and the Cinque Port volunteers were disbanded the following June.

In 1807 Rye suffered a terrible tragedy. A local vessel called the *Chiswell*, with a cargo of malt belonging to Mr Lewis Meryon, was lost with all hands. She was waiting under Dungeness for the tide to help her into Rye harbour when a fierce gale sprang up in the night. She was never seen again. Not a body, or piece of wreckage was ever picked up.

In 1833 the Corporation built the sea wall which encloses the town and Town Salts, providing Ryers with unique recreation grounds which are still in constant use. Ten years later the railway from London had reached Ashford and, in 1845, it was proposed to extend it across the Marsh to Rye and Hastings. By the end of the first half of the nineteenth century the first railway train reached Rye with great civic rejoicing. The line is still open and, in spite of many threats of closure, still does good work.

In 1859 there was another scare of a French invasion under Napoleon III and Rye, as usual, was among the first to hold a public meeting which carried unanimously that "a Volunteer Rifle Corps" be formed in the town.

The history books - particularly Leopold Vidler's *A New History of Rye* - occasionally give some startling and fascinating details of what occurred in the town during this century of political upheaval. There were indeed some awkward cases following the Parliamentary Reform Act of 1832. "Bribery, corruption and drunkenness, the usual results of taking one's politics too seriously, were rife and practised by both parties," says Vidler, for instance.

Lighter relief, although it was not very amusing for Ryers, is recorded from the same source. The year was 1881. In February, the town suffered from an extraordinarily high tide, running to 20 ft. 9 ins. at Rye Harbour. The sea broke through the wall at Rock Channel and flooded all the low-lying parts to the south and west of the town. "It is said that the smell from the dead worms on the Salts, after it had receded, was most offensive and the grass took some years to recover."

There were splendid celebrations on the occasion of Queen Victoria's Jubilee in June 1887. The day opened with a peal on the church bells and a breakfast, given by the Mayor to the leading inhabitants of the town, was followed by a Thanksgiving Service in the church. At noon, a free dinner was given in the Agricultural Hall to all householders. Later, all the children of Rye walked in procession through the town to the Salts where the Mayor presented each one with a Jubilee medal, a threepenny piece and a bun! There were sports on the Salts, a great bonfire when darkness fell on a glorious day and a Town Ball at the then Cinque Ports Hotel. Later in the year avenues of trees were planted on the North Salts in honour of the Jubilee.

In 1888, Rye Regatta was revived and held at the Fishmarket at the time of the spring tides. By the end of the century Britain was at war again - this time with the Boers in South Africa - and many citizens volunteered for service overseas and were duly honoured on their safe return.

Nothing of note is recorded of the town during the next few years. Then, in 1902, the Cinque Ports' right of attendance at the coronation of King Edward VII was granted and Rye claimed, and was also granted, her ancient right of attendance. The Mayor and another representative attended Westminster Abbey with the other Barons of the Cinque Ports.

At midnight on 4th August 1914, Great Britain declared war on Germany and the 5th Battalion (Cinque Ports) Royal Sussex Regiment was at once recalled from camp and sent to Dover Castle, passing through Rye on its way. Again, volunteers of all ages from the Ancient Town flocked to the colours. The Battalion suffered heavy losses in May 1915 and in March of that critical year there was an air raid on Rye Harbour. Three bombs were dropped but did no damage beyond shifting some shingle. It is difficult to believe today but it was suggested at the time that the enemy mistook our muddy Rother for the mouth of the Thames!

It is typical of Rye that one of the Corporation's first actions in 1919 after the Armistice was to pass a resolution that Germany should bear the whole cost of the war!

The restless and disillusioned twenties slipped by. Rye began to grow. New roads of little houses appeared outside the ancient walls and electricity came to the town from Hastings. Some of its old industries were beginning to decay but Rye was beginning to be discovered by authors and artists who brought a new kind of trade. Perhaps this affection and respect of so many visitors has helped to keep alive Rye's old craft of the potter, for there are now four Potteries in the town exporting to many parts of the world. We know that potters were working on Rye Hill in the thirteenth century and the Museum has some remarkable exhibits of the craft.

On 15th November 1928, Rye was suddenly in the news again under most tragic circumstances. The facts of this shocking tragedy, which surely will always rank high amongst the memories and records of Rye's 'Vanished Men' are as follows: on the morning of this grim November day a fierce gale was raging in the Channel. Only those who have experienced a south-westerly in Rye Bay at this time of year can have any conception of the mountainous seas and force of the wind. During the morning of this fateful day the Rye Harbour lifeboat, the *Mary Stanford,* under the command of Coxswain Head, with a crew of 16, was launched in response to a call for help from a Latvian vessel - the *S. S. Alice* of Riga. By an ironic stroke of fate this boat was rescued by another lifeboat stationed further east along the coast and, although a message of recall was sent to Rye Harbour, it arrived too late. We shall never know the feelings of our brave crew when they had to turn back in those terrifying seas without knowing whether the *Alice* had sunk without a trace. They would surely have known that their loved ones were waiting for them on the drenched shingle beach towards which they were struggling, exhausted, through the tempestuous seas, for home. They were indeed within reach of help when their boat capsized and not one man was saved. This scene is sympathetically and beautifully recorded in one of the modern memorial windows in Winchelsea church. Hours later their lifeless bodies were washed ashore, and there were not many homes in Rye Harbour which were not bereaved.

The Mayor at this time was Leopold Amon Vidler, author of *A New History of Rye,* which has been constantly referred to and acknowledged in these pages. His personal account of this tragedy is moving and graphic. It so happens that for nearly eighteen years he had been the Honorary Secretary of the Rye Branch of the Royal National Lifeboat Institution and so it was his responsibility to get medical aid, report to London, visit the coast and see the dead bodies washed ashore. And that very night he was wakened by a loud knocking at his door and handed by a reporter of the now deceased *Daily Chronicle,* a cheque for £250 to open a Relief Fund for the bereaved dependents. I quote now from his account of this tragic incident: "But the inquest had to be attended and no one present will ever forget the crowded wooden hut at Camber where, in a howling gale which threatened every moment to carry off the roof, the coroner, surrounded by a circle of tense and grief-stricken relatives, held his inquiry into this awful drama of the sea."

Donations to the fund poured in and after two months, when the fund was closed, the magnificent sum of £34,455 had been received from over 12,000 subscribers. The R.N.L.I. then closed the station but at Rye Harbour today you may see, displayed unobtrusively, a board giving the names and records of service and lives saved by the Lifeboats of Rye.

And so we come to the war through which some readers of these words will have lived. Although this coastline, with flat marsh land behind, was prepared for and guarded against an invasion which never came, Rye itself suffered from aerial attack. Strange that through the centuries, this little British bastion which had frequently suffered invasion from the sea, should now face attack from the air.

Ryers seem to have had a very uncomfortable time during these years. It would, I suppose, have been possible to ferret out some official information as to the actual number of direct hits from enemy aircraft and flying bombs and somewhere there must be a record of those civilians who lost their lives or who were injured. But I have preferred to talk to one or two residents who actually lived in the town during those vital years.

I spent a few days of convalescence with my wife at the Hope Anchor in February 1940. I believe the hotel itself was occupied by the Royal Sussex Regiment as we slept in an annexe in Watchbell Street. The town was blacked out of course and I remember that coal fires were a great comfort and that somebody commented that "Ryers didn't hold with coal rationing down their way." It seemed tactful to refrain from further questioning or surprise! There were no air raids while we were there but I remember that the glorious news came over the radio of the capture of the *Altmark* and the rescue of nearly 300 British prisoners. Those were the days when Britain took action first and answered questions after the operation was complete!

I am indebted to Mr Charles Tomlin, who for 21 years was employed as butler-valet to E. F. Benson when he lived in Lamb House and who later acted as caretaker. He was an Air Raid Warden in Rye throughout the war. Those of us of that particular vintage do not find it easy to remember the most unpleasant facts and figures of the long war years. It is as well that we should recall more easily the comradeship, courage and unselfishness that were more obvious then than now. Mr Tomlin certainly does that.

There seems no doubt that a very large number of houses in Rye received some damage during that time. Most of this was the result of hit-and-run raids, particularly from enemy bombers on their way home. Danger was more acute in daytime because warnings of approaching aircraft were naturally very short. True, Ryers have plenty of cellars but there was rarely any time to stand gossiping in the streets!

The worst damage, apart from the destruction of the famous Garden Room at Lamb House in West Street about which more later, seems to be as follows: three smallish cottages on the east side of Church Square by the Ypres Tower were completely destroyed. They stood more or less in the position of the bigger modern houses now set well back from the road. Needless to add, the Ypres Tower withstood anything Hitler could do, although this bomb was probably the one responsible for damaging the Wesleyan Chapel a few yards away. Strand House and other houses in the Strand were also badly damaged; small houses at the bottom of the Mint, among them. In those days there were two wooden houses at the top of Trader's Passage and they also were destroyed and a woman killed. Some men working on the roof of the already damaged Ship Hotel were killed in a second raid.

Another very unpleasant incident was the complete destruction of the cinema by a direct hit from a hit-and-run raider. A relief manager who had only taken over that day was killed. Had the bomb fallen a few hours later, when an afternoon showing had been planned, the death roll might have been very heavy. Mr Tomlin reminds me that Rye was allowed to rebuild the cinema immediately after the war as a special favour!

A typical act of German warfare was the machine-gunning by another 'hit and runner' of a small fishing boat out in the bay. Two men were killed and their surviving companion, Charlie Locke, brought the boat home single-handed and was subsequently awarded the M.B.E. The action of a typical Ryer!

Rye Harbour was also severely attacked in a daylight raid and lives were lost in this incident. The destruction of the steel railway bridge over the Rother was attempted but the bombs fell wide. Some unexploded bombs also fell in the town itself.

Later, the Doodle Bugs were a nuisance. They arrived virtually without warning, although the R. A. F. made valiant attempts to shoot them down over the Channel. During this time our planes were also constantly searching for launching sites and the secret weapon about which Hitler was boasting.

While through all these weary years Rye itself suffered, there must have been tremendous activity on the Marsh and Pett Level beyond Winchelsea to the west. Enemy landings were certainly expected here. Some of the level was flooded. Defences against marauding parachutists were erected on the Marsh and troops were stationed on the Kent Ditch to guard a radar station.

The outskirts of Rye, beyond the town walls, also suffered from flying bombs. Many houses on the Udimore Road were damaged and one man was killed. There were guns stationed below Cadborough Cliff and so, once again, Rye was in the front line. We know now that not many miles away, across the bay at Dungeness, oil was flowing through P.L.U.T.O. - the pipeline-under-the-ocean - for allied troops in France. It is also rumoured that there was a subterranean oil storage depot under the sand dunes of Camber. Could the Germans possibly have known this?

So in many ways Rye was, as always, in the front line of defence and it seems as if Ryers took it all in their stride. Time has mellowed the scars of aerial bombardment. The Ypres Tower, for many years the Town Museum, still stands four-square facing the narrow seas and the Landgate still guards the town from the road to London but you will be welcomed if you come that way now.

With the end of the war the world was changed and some of us were aware that the old order had gone forever. Except for the damage inflicted by the bombing, the fundamental Rye was still the same. The noble church still crowned the hill and dominated the town's profile. The Quarter Boys on each side of its ancient clock still jerkily struck their bells three times an hour. The gulls still circled and cried above the sheep-dotted Marsh and Camber Castle squatted where Henry VIII set it to guard the mouth of the harbour.

Rye has its ghosts and we shall hear more of them as we explore their haunts in later chapters but before we say farewell to Rye's 'Vanished Men' we must record its literary associations and attractions for artists and authors. First of these was John Fletcher, the dramatist and collaborator with both Shakespeare and Beaumont. He was born in Rye in 1579 at the old house at the top of Lion Street which is still known as Fletcher's House and serves excellent food and drink. John was the son of Richard Fletcher who was not a native of Rye and it seems that he left the town with his family in 1581. John's memories of Rye must have been scanty. He never referred to the town in any of his writings but he was certainly baptized in Rye Church on 20th December, 1579.

We have seen that the first Samuel Jeake was a typical Ryer and a man of many accomplishments including his *Charters of the Cinque Ports, Two Ancient Towns and Their Members,* published in 1728. Then

LAMB HOUSE

JOHN
ALLSUP

there was William Holloway who wrote his famous *History of the Town and Port of Rye* in 1847 and, of course, Leopold Amon Vidler whose *A New History of Rye* is referred to constantly in this book.

Probably the most famous of all the town's literary inhabitants was Henry James who lived in Lamb House from 1897 until he died in 1916. He loved the house and town and worked every morning in the separate Garden Room which, as has been recorded, was destroyed by enemy action in 1940. Only very rarely did he leave Rye and during his tenure one of his greatest friends was the English novelist E. F. Benson. Henry James bequeathed Lamb House to his nephew of the same name who lived in New York but Benson and his brother, Robert Hugh, took over the house. When the owner died, Lamb House was given to the National Trust and the next tenant was a relation of Henry James, H. Montgomery Hyde, whose *Story of Lamb House, Rye* is now out of print. This writer left Rye many years ago and the literary tradition was continued by Rumer Godden, the novelist and writer for children who lived there until 1974 before moving to another house in the town. *[Ed. Rumer Godden died in 1998.]*

What is now called Jeake's House (and was formerly Jeake's Storehouse) in Mermaid Street also has literary associations. The American poet and novelist Conrad Aiken lived there in the 1920s. These years were an era when writers and artists and such creative men and women were more important than television personalities. We read that among those who visited Rye at this time were T. S. Eliot, Julian Huxley and Dame Laura Knight. Robert Nichols the poet and Paul Nash the artist also lived in Rye for a time.

Today *[Ed. 1976]*, Patric Dickinson, another poet lives in Church Square and Eric Whelpton the popular travel writer and his artist wife Barbara Crocker live in Trader's Passage.

Rye attracts such distinguished people but when we consider the 'Story of Vanished Men' it is obvious that those who have given their best to the town are true Ryers. Nobody served Rye in a civic sense as did those who lived in the town. Look at the list of Mayors: Grebell, Lamb, Vidler, Meryon, Gasson, for instance. This honour also came to E. F. Benson, M.B.E. in 1934 who was not a native of the town. The names live on. Through peace and war and the time of the Rotten Boroughs, Rye rarely failed to honour those who had served the 'Ancient Town' with distinction.

And so, with some humility, I end this chapter with the Reverend A. T. Saville's concluding words to his lecture, 'Ancient Rye', which was delivered to the Rye Mutual Improvement Society on 14th January 1890:

"Rye did great things in the past, because its sons did their utmost, there was nothing slipshod, sleepy or half-hearted. With both hands earnestly they defended the old town against mighty odds, with both hands earnestly they fed the hungry, clothed the naked, and housed the homeless. If they built a church, a castle or a gateway, their utmost strength and skill were put forward. Hence the monuments of their industry stand today. And if we are to do anything great, and strong and lasting, something which will live when we are forgotten, we must put forth our uttermost, and be as thorough as our fathers."

THE LANDGATE

JOHN ALLCUP

Chapter Three:

Around the Town

The First Journey

We now explore the Ancient Town and I suggest that our journeys be leisurely. Most readers will probably come by car but during the holiday months of June, July and August in particular, the difficulties of parking in the narrow streets are acute. Rye is not yet by-passed, but as the only way to appreciate the town is to stroll and stop and stare, I must assume that you have left your vehicle on the outskirts or arrived by train or bus.

There are five approaches to Rye by road and from four I suggest a walk but you may prefer to wander as you will. I want to show you Rye through my eyes, so that my words will revive your memories and bring you back again. I have known this town for nearly sixty years and I believe that you too will fall under its spell. There is a subtle magic about Rye. Not just because it is old and historic and a part of Britain's heritage - more than that. It is lively, welcoming, beautiful and, in some inexplicable way, brings the past into the present and shares this experience with those who treat it with respect. If you feel like this about it you will return. It may be years but there will come a day when you will recall with nostalgia your first glimpse of Rye's red roofs clinging tenaciously to its little hill. You will remember too the views of the distant sea, the muddy river with the gulls circling and crying above the Fishmarket and the prospect of the grassy levels thick with sheep, which open up before you from so many vantage points. My suggestions for exploring the town, street by street, are not arbitrary. The index to this book will help you to identify what you see.

The most dramatic approach is from the centuries-old road from London (A268) bringing you through Peasmarsh and Rye Foreign (where many of the Huguenot refugees settled) to Playden. There is nothing special about the latter except its delightful name but just after passing the Rye Memorial Care Centre on the right, the tree-lined road drops sharply and you will notice, on the other side of the road, the town sign welcoming you to Rye. Suddenly, on your left you will see a row of Victorian houses where the Military Road from across the Marsh joins the A268. Over the railway bridge and then you must turn left. There is a car park here and another a little further on after turning right on to the Hastings road. Leave the car in one of these and walk back to the road junction, turn left into the narrow street called Landgate and, in front of you, is the massive medieval gateway. This should be your first entrance to the town. Walk under it on the left-hand pavement, remembering that this is a one-way street with traffic approaching behind you.

You are now within the walls and the history of this great medieval gateway is recorded on a metal plaque above you. The legend reads: *This ancient monument was built in 1329 when Edward III made grants for further fortifying the town, and of the four gateways built, this is the only existing one. It has a chamber over the arch and two towers. There were gates, a portcullis and a drawbridge.* From this description we can assume that the town, at this time, was also guarded by a moat, or ditch.

Look across the street now and you will see, close to the western tower of the gateway, the entrance to a rather gloomy alley. This narrow passage, now marked as Turkey Cock Lane, was formerly Tower Lane and has the reputation of being haunted. We shall visit it on another walk and its story shall then be told again.

Turn up the hill now. You will pass a shop which was once a forge and then some wide, gently-sloping steps leading down to Fishmarket Road, the Town Salts and the two car parks. This entrance to a small town and the prospect opening out to the south-east is completely unexpected. A town set on a hill is often dramatic. Sometimes I am reminded of the hill villages of Tuscany and of the bigger Umbrian town of Orvieto, which rises so abruptly from the plain.

But Rye, now deserted by the sea, is typically British and, from where you stand looking down on the fishing boats and across the Rother to the Marsh, you will realize that it only *seems* to stand high. The illusion exists because most of the surrounding land is below sea level and the effect is emphasized by the clarity of the light.

The street is labelled Eastcliff but is sometimes known as Hilder's Cliff. The first large house on the right dates from the early eighteenth century. It is now known as Tower House, although it once performed the function of a private club called the Dormy House. The next building on that side of the road is the Rye Lodge Hotel. This was once a Girls' Collegiate School.

As we climb the gentle hill the panorama unfolds. The local authorities have thoughtfully provided two 'lookout' terraces and you will notice that the first of these bears the name of 'John Symonds Vidler, 1914.' From here you can look down on the town's bowling green and enjoy a better view of the fishing boats on the Rother, which is much more spectacular at high tide. It will probably be clear enough for you to see the Dungeness Nuclear Power Station and the pylons striding inland across the Marsh. The white sandy dunes and beaches of Camber are clearly visible on the other side of the river.

Just opposite a small house called 'Gris Nez' a flight of steep steps leads down to Fishmarket Road. Better down than up! The cliff is precipitous here. A few yards further on and you must pause

47

in a bigger 'lookout' terrace which is always crowded with visitors in the summer. Here is a telescope - and very efficient too, because with its help you can see Dungeness Lighthouse, the noble tower of Lydd Church which was badly damaged in the last war and, on a fine day, the white cliffs of Dover. Without its help, you are offered an amazing view of the backs of the houses perched high on the edge of the cliff on your right. Below you the children's playground stands on the Town Salts which were covered by the sea as late as the beginning of the nineteenth century. Few small towns can boast better public playgrounds than these smooth, green levels. Beyond them is the Fishmarket. If the tide is flowing you may see a few boats coming up to their moorings and it is good to see them and to know that fishing is still practised here, although the fleet is dwindling.

The road swings sharply right now into the High Street. Don't miss the remarkable shop on the opposite side of the road and note that the building next to it bears the name 'Hilder' on the pediment below the roof. There were several Hilders in Rye's municipal history in Victorian days.

This entrance into the main street is another surprise. In shopping hours it will be busy but the first impression is that almost every building is different. At this end there are no modern chain stores but a brave array of small businesses. On the left you will pass - not pass, I hope, if it is open - Rye's Art Gallery, comprising the Stormont Gallery and the Easton Rooms, where various exhibitions from the work of local artists and others are displayed; access to the latter may also be had from East Street. It is typical of Rye that a town of only about 4,000 inhabitants can keep such an excellent institution alive. Close by, on the opposite side of the street, is the seventeenth century Monastery Restaurant with the delightful and secluded Friary gardens behind it.

Before leaving the tantalizing High Street, notice the butcher's shop with nostalgic brass fittings and, before turning left, pause at the corner to admire the splendid Apothecary's Shop with its magnificent bow windows. East Street is my favourite way up to the citadel round the church. There are not many shops in this street but a few paces after turning the corner is an entrance on the left to a private lane or courtyard. In this is another door, on a higher level, to the Easton Rooms of Rye Art Gallery and an entrancing glimpse, at the end of the cul-de-sac, across the Salts to the wooded hills towards Iden.

Note the variety of types of red brick and whitewashed walls in East Street. Every house is different and distinct. On the right, near the top, see the unusual sign of the Union Inn.

Almost opposite are three tall houses, the first of which was once the Vicarage. It is now a hotel. Next is Cannon House. Note the heavy oak door in which is set a panel with an inscription which reads: *This oak plank originally formed part of a 14th century Prison door.* The name of the prison is not given. The Ypres Tower perhaps? Between this house and the next, which is called La Rochelle, is a narrow alley leading to a precipitous flight of crumbling steps down to Fishmarket Road. Not even for the sake of my readers have I ever risked this dangerous journey and I doubt if this way down has been used for years. Walk carefully to the top of them to look at the view and at the backs of the houses built on the edge of the cliff on your right.

'La Rochelle' reminds us of the Huguenots who soon repaid, with their industry and craftsmanship, the hospitality of Ryers. In this house, as a wall plaque proclaims, lived Paul Nash the artist, from 1899 to 1946.

Turn right into Market Street, which is one of the pleasantest, and widest, thoroughfares in Rye. Pleasant now but not always so, because it was the site of the town's market and butchery years ago.

The first house on the left is the elegant Durrant House Hotel with Georgian facade and a few yards farther on is the famous Flushing Inn which is one of the oldest buildings in Rye and certainly worth inspecting. It is timber-framed, dating from the fifteenth century, built on an earlier stone base. The medieval cellar is enormous but its most notable feature is a sixteenth century wall-painting which was only accidentally discovered in 1905. It is now preserved behind glass and can be inspected in the dining room. It is a remarkable specimen of a mural incorporating foliage, flowers, beasts and birds with heraldic designs including the crest of Queen Jane Seymour. Not much evidence exists of the use of the Flushing as an inn although there is no doubt about its antiquity. At one time it was owned by the murderer, Breads, who had his butchery at the back. Certainly it was used by smugglers. It is said that it had a footway up the east cliff at the bottom of which boats could beach. Could this be the precipitous flight of broken steps by the side of La Rochelle? The cellars would have been invaluable and contraband could have been brought along this route into the very heart of the town.

Another building used for the same purpose is almost opposite. Cross the street and look at the very old bakery which is one of many in the town. This one is known as Ye Olde Tucke Shoppe. The title does not suggest that this building is believed to date from the fourteenth century and has been baking bread, which is a delight to all Ryers and those who live near enough to shop in the town, in the original oven built in 1750. But that is not all. The chimney in the bakehouse has a wheel at the top which was used by smugglers to hoist kegs of brandy up to the attics above. Note now that no house on this side of the street is detached. It is said that contraband delivered to the bakehouse - possibly from the Flushing Inn - could be transferred through the adjoining attics of the innocent looking houses on this side of Market Street to the Union Inn in East Street. A fascinating supposition but no evidence seems to exist that this theory has been tested.

Before we leave Market Street by the narrow, cobbled lane almost opposite the bakery, we must look at the Town Hall. This is a most attractive building designed by a London master mason and built in 1743. The lower storey on the ground floor is arcaded, giving access to the market space. There is a large Court Room on the floor above featuring a list on the wall of all the Mayors of Rye. This Hall is the successor of several buildings which served the borough and is crowned with a cupola in which hung the Jurats' Bell used to summon the Jurats to the Quarter Sessions.

Although the Town Hall is not generally open to the public, some of its treasures can be seen by special arrangement. These treasures are unique and extremely valuable. The magnificent silver-gilt maces were presented to the Corporation in 1767. Originally, Rye had been governed by the King's Bailiff and the Mayor. As time passed they became predominant until, in 1704, the Corporation assumed the dual role, with the result that the Mayor became entitled to the two maces. One of the smaller maces is dated 1570. The Mayor's Chain of Office is of solid gold can also be seen. The interior of the building has been redecorated and the fine Court Room is well worth seeing.

Back now to the narrow, cobbled lane which will lead us into Church Square, the Ypres Tower and the famous Gungarden, with another superb view of the levels and the Rother making its way to the sea.

This short, narrow lane is of considerable interest. Although officially now part of Church Square it was once called Pump Street. There is no name plate, at the time of writing, on the walls of either building at its entrance from Market Street. The left-hand side features a few delightful and varied houses. The first building on the left might be the site of the butchery of the murderer Breads whose skull is still kept in the Town Hall. You may have seen a replica of the skull in the Heritage Centre. But the most interesting feature is the brick waterhouse or cistern, built in the eighteenth century, actually in the churchyard. Experts claim that its beautiful oval shape with tiled roof is probably unique in England. Rye has

PVMP STREET

JOHN ALLSUP

never been short of water, which was obtained from wells under the north-east cliffs and springs outside the town walls but until the building of this storage tank, the main waterhouse was at the foot of Conduit Hill. The idea of storing water at the highest point of the town had obvious advantages. New, two-inch elm pipes were laid from the main reservoir and the water pumped up to the waterhouse. The lengthy notes referring to the construction of this ambitious and worthy project are recorded on a metal plaque on the side of the building. I particularly like that recorded under - *June 10, 1736. 7/- to be paid to Edward Wilson, Vicar, for damage to churchyard by digging reservoir, if he will receive it.*

A few steps further and you will see for the first time, the magnificent flying buttresses at the east end of the church. We shall visit this historic building later but these buttresses are very fine. The street on our right is part of Church Square and leads into the superb Watchbell Street. The bright, pleasant building opposite is the reconstructed Methodist Church, formerly the Methodist Sunday School. The original chapel was built in 1814 and almost totally destroyed in a bombing raid in 1942; the site of the original chapel is now occupied by the Rectory. I have always thought that this place epitomizes the very spirit of Rye. Here, where the sea once washed the base of the cliff below still stands one of the oldest buildings in the town.

It is known as the Ypres Tower and was built in 1250 by order of Henry III to fortify the town. Notice particularly the four corner towers. Each of these is 40 ft. high and the walls between 3 and 4 feet thick. No wonder that Hitler was unable to do more than blow off a red-tiled roof in an air raid in September 1942. In 1837 an exercise yard was added, together with four more cells and a woman's tower, to the east of the main buildings.

It is fitting that this noble monument to the town's history for many years housed Rye's Museum which was founded in 1928 by Leopold Vidler, Mayor of Rye and historian, to whose work grateful reference has already been made. It was originally housed in Battery House close by, which was also destroyed by enemy action but many of the exhibits were salvaged and may be seen today. In 1975 it was given the Regional Award (South-east England) in the 'National Heritage Museum of the Year Awards.' Today *[Ed. 1999]* some of the artefacts are being moved to the museum's additional premises in East Street. Every visitor to Rye would do well to visit the Museum when it reopens.

The Ypres Tower itself has just reopened after a period of refurbishment. It is true that, at the height of the tourist season, there is not much elbow room in a building that was intended for defence and later used as a prison. There is also a parapet above a small green in the medieval style which was once the exercise yard. From here there is an inspiring view of the Town Salts and the Marsh beyond.

It is refreshing, after visiting the Tower, to stroll into the Gungarden a few yards away. Again, even in its old age, we are at once aware of Rye's former commanding situation. The town has made the best of this delightful vantage point and we now get a fine view of the Rother making its way to the sea after being fed by the combined rivers of Tillingham and Brede. The industrial development on the way to Rye Harbour is mercifully blurred by distance and the shadowy bulk of Camber Castle is away to the right, with Winchelsea on its green hill even further west. On a clear day, with the aid of another telescope, it should be possible to see the chalk cliffs beyond Folkestone.

There were guns here of course, ever since the days of Elizabeth I. This monarch, who did not forget the part played by the ships of the Cinque Ports in the defeat of the Spanish Armada, presented Rye with six brass guns ornamented with the arms of Spain. History does not record what happened to these priceless souvenirs or where they are now. *[Ed. Over the years there have been a succession of various cannon; in 1980 three mock cannon were manufactured in Rye and*

*presented to the Queen Mother in celebration of her 80ᵗʰ birthday. These now
stand in the Gungarden in place of the original brass guns.]*

Turn your back to the sea for another view of the Ypres Tower
and against the rear wall of the Gungarden you will see an
enormous anchor which was trawled up by a local fishing boat
from Rye Bay some years ago. It is tempting to suggest that this is
another trophy from the defeated Armada but there is no evidence
to support this.

The Gungarden is a perfect place for a picnic on a sunny day.
A few yards away, approached by steps leading down to Fishmarket
Road, is an inn known as the Ypres Castle, with a pleasant garden.
Directly below, on the banks of the combined waters of the
Tillingham and Brede, is where Rye's ship building yards once
supplied boats for the Cinque Ports fleet.

The Second Journey

As a contrast to the first spectacular entrance to the town from
the north, through wooded and pastoral country, we now take a
route from the east.- The main road from Folkestone (A259) crosses
the flat Walland Marsh soon after leaving New Romney but there
is another, not so busy, road worth trying. This is the B2075 from
Lydd, alongside the Firing Ranges (Danger Area) and then
alongside the sea wall to Camber, in which there is no need to
linger. After leaving the Holiday Camps the road runs close to
Rye's famous Golf Links. The Rother, on its way to the sea is on
the left and the B2075 soon joins the A259 at a hamlet called East
Guldeford (pronounced Gillford).

Almost as soon as you turn left at this road junction you will see
Rye on its hill. You can pull in on a lay-by and enjoy this dramatic
view of the town ahead and to the country to the south-west

beyond it. On the horizon are the Fairlight Hills which stretch from Hastings to Cliff End at the edge of Pett Level. The tower on the highest point is that of Fairlight Church which dominates this stretch of coast and is a famous landmark for sailors in the Channel.

On our right, on the other side of the road, are the wooded cliffs below the village of Playden and it is easy to see that the sea once beat against them. A bridge, named after Lord Monkbretton, carries the A259 over the Rother which is quite spectacular here when the tide is full. As it ebbs, the slimy, muddy banks are exposed and not even the town's greatest enthusiast would declare that it is a beautiful river. But it is Rye's own river and, with the help of its two tributaries, the Brede and the Tillingham, it links the ancient port with the sea. At the time of writing [Ed. 1976] there are still fishing boats moored at the Fishmarket which is bounded on the town side by the Salts and Recreation Grounds on which we looked down, from Hilder's Cliff.

Although it is not possible to see the exact spot, there is a special point of interest on the left just before crossing the Monkbretton Bridge. Here, a few yards from the road, was the terminus of a remarkable little railway which linked Rye with the Golf Links and was eventually extended to Camber Sands. Two coaches were used, hauled originally by a steam locomotive known as the Rye and Camber Tram. The single line track was still in use until the outbreak of war in 1939 and I remember the thrill of travelling on it as a boy, at about 10 m.p.h. from Rye, out to the delectable sand dunes of Camber.

The A259 turns sharp left soon after crossing the bridge and here there is an excellent car park. Directly opposite the entrance is a slope with shallow steps at one side. This is your way up into the town. When halfway up, turn and look back across the Salts to the Fishmarket and to the masts of the fishing boats.

At the top of the slope you will find yourself on Hilder's Cliff where you started to explore Rye on our first journey. Turn down the hill this time, noticing the Old Forge, now an antique pine furniture shop. Cross the road to the entrance to Turkey Cock Lane, already mentioned. The truth is that this end of it is now little more than a rather squalid alley, associated with a ghost story that has stood the test of time. The Town Wall must have stood where the backs of the houses in Tower Street are now on our right and, beyond that, would have been the defensive ditch. No doubt the 'Lane' was cobbled and wider than it is now for, as we shall see, it is only about 200 yards from the Augustinian Friary which was built in the late fourteenth century.

The legend of the haunting has been retold with various embellishments many times but because Leopold Vidler's version in his *New History of Rye* seems to me to be the best of them all I reprint it here, as written, with the permission of his son, Dr Alec Vidler.

"In after years, the following legend arose in connection with the Friary. It is said that one of the Friars, by name Cantator, who was gifted with a very fine voice and sang in the choir, had the misfortune, considering his vows, to fall in love with a very beautiful girl, by name Amanda, who lived in the old Tower House nearby. Matters between them went further than they should have done and it came to the ears of the authorities who, after the fashion of those days, buried these two unfortunate people alive. Of course, they could not, after such treatment, rest quietly in their grave and Amanda was frequently seen fluttering, white faced and white robed, in the windows of her father's house, now reputed to be haunted, while Cantator strutted up and down the lane in the form of a turkey cock, gobbling his old love songs to her. However, in the year 1850, the South Eastern Railway, while digging foundations, came across their skeletons, still clasped in each other's arms, and again the authorities were approached and this time it was decided to give them Christian burial, and never since have they been seen or heard by mortal eyes or ears."

The old Tower House was probably on the site of the eighteen century building on Hilder's Cliff which for many years was called the Dormy House but has since reverted to its original name. It is possible, at the end of this depressing alley, to realize how near the building must have been to the Friary. The lovely Amanda might easily have been captivated by the melodious voice of the young friar singing in the garden of his monastic home – and walls can be scaled by ardent lovers!

Conduit Hill is the steepest cobbled street in Rye. As its name suggests, there must have been a well or cistern at the foot of the slope which is also the site of another of the town's fortified entrances - the narrow Postern Gate, for pedestrians only. The much-renovated Victorian building on our immediate left, as we stand at the end of Turkey Cock Lane, is the old Congregational Church and Halls which were built chiefly through the energies of my grandfather who accepted an invitation to the charge of the small Congregational Church in Rye. He had worked for some years as a missionary in the South Seas and settled in Rye in 1878 where he remained for 27 years. He began his ministry in an old building on the north side of Watchbell Street but it was soon obvious that this accommodation was too small for the growing congregations. The present site was then chosen and the new church was built and cleared of debt. The Halls for the growing Sunday Schools soon followed.

In 1973 these premises were purchased by the Rye Community Centre Association with the help of the East Sussex Education Committee and the Department of Education and Science. The Centre was redecorated, rewired and installed with central heating and a new stage and proscenium. Although the late Reverend A. T. Saville might regret that the buildings he so enthusiastically built for the Congregationalists of Rye no longer serve their original purpose, I feel sure he would approve their present use and, with pride, his grandson quotes some words written at the time of his death in 1915: "He was everybody's friend: a true father of the community, taking his part in public affairs, the wise councillor of many beyond his own flock, and of them the greatly trusted and beloved leader."

It is worth walking a few steps up the hill from here and looking at what is left of the Friary – wrongly called the Monastery - and now one of Rye's justifiably famous Potteries. This is not the original Augustinian Friary, for that was below the east cliff and was undermined by the sea in the middle of the fourteenth century. What is left of the present building was built about 1380 - probably soon after the disastrous attack by the French on the town in 1377. It is possible to climb the steep flight of steps to the pottery show room. Although there is a gate close by to the garden, this belongs to the Monastery Restaurant in the High Street.

Walk back now down the hill, cross the road where the Postern Gate once stood, into the delightfully named Rope Walk. Vidler tells us that in 1711 Thomas Grebell was again made Mayor and "during his year of office was granted permission to set up posts in Rope Walk to make ropes." A short way along Rope Walk is a car park which is really part of the large area given up to Rye's Market Place. A Cattle Market is held here every Wednesday and the entire space from Rope Walk to the Station Approach is given up to the General Market ('Petticoat Lane' comes to Rye) every Thursday.

Walk back now to the top of Rope Walk and turn right into Cinque Ports Street. On the left is a small car park, at the back of which is the best remaining stretch of the old Town Wall, giving a good indication of its height and strength. Opposite, where Rye's cinema once stood, new shops and a Police Station have now been built. The entrance to the Station Approach is on the right and, as this is also the Bus Station, it is a lively, busy place - particularly on market days. The Railway Station is attractive in its Victorian way. On 29th October 1850, the Town Clerk invited the inhabitants to join the Mayor and Corporation, to welcome the Chairman and Directors of the South Eastern Railway Company to inspect the new bridge over the Rother and this station. Ironically, only 120 years later the station and the railway between Hastings and Ashford was swooning under the kiss of death. It was reprieved in 1974.

I like Rye's Railway Station. I have many happy memories of exciting arrivals and nostalgic departures. But we must leave the station and take the street up the hill to the High Street, opposite the Station Approach, with its patient queues waiting for buses. This narrow, one-way street is called Market Road. It seems to belong more to Rye's visitors than to Ryers but it is always lively. Halfway up on the left is a modern development of flats and houses named after a previous Mayor of Rye.

On this tour we turn left at the top of Market Road into the High Street. The second shop is one of the most attractive bookshops I know. The building boasted a library over 200 years ago and somewhere at the rear of the shop, now thick with books for every taste, there was once a printing press. It is now named The Martello Bookshop.

When you leave the shop turn left. You will see how gently the street curves and how attractive the buildings are on each side of it. You need not stroll far before reaching two of the most notable buildings in Rye. The first, on the left, is the redbrick building known as the Old Grammar School. It was built by Thomas Peacocke in 1636, as we read in an earlier chapter. Experts maintain that the brickwork and classical features of the frontage would not be likely to be the handiwork of local labour and indeed it does look rather foreign. Mr Bagley, in his official Guide Book, suggests that a journeying workman from Flanders might be responsible and this may well be, as Rye had a direct trade with that country at this time. 'Peacocke's' has been immortalized by Thackeray in his unfinished novel *Denis Duval*. He calls it Pocock's. It has not been used as a school for years but Rye's new Comprehensive School has been named after its founder. The unusual facade of the old 'Peacocke's' is safe now but the interior is put to commercial use.

Opposite is the George Hotel - a big building with a Georgian front. A beautiful Assembly Room with a Musicians' Gallery was added in 1818 and many interior alterations have been made since. There are still signs of a much older Tudor building on this site. Originally the George was in Market Street but moved here early in the eighteenth century. The pillared porch is particularly attractive and there is still a yard which would once have been used by coaches.

The George stands at the corner of Lion Street which will lead us up the hill to the Church and to the 'Citadel' which is the most fascinating part of Rye. The narrow street itself has some attractive shops. In the season it is crowded with visitors either waiting to watch the gilded Quarter Boys on the church tower strike one of the three 'quarters' - they do not strike the hour - and almost certainly to take photographs. At the top, on the left, is Market Street and the Town Hall which we have already seen and, opposite, the entrance to the Public Library - once a school - and the Further Education Centre. Neither of these buildings is of architectural merit but hereabouts is the site of the old Red Lion Inn. Mr Bagley in his *Old Inns & Ale Houses of Rye*, tells us that between 1709 and the 1870s, it was the town's third major inn, until it was burned down. The book illustrates two delightful bill-heads, one of which proudly proclaims, 'A Coach to and from London, every Tuesday and Friday. Neat Post-Chaise.'

The next two houses are obviously Tudor. They both serve citizens and visitors with refreshment and are well placed close to the church to do so. The second is known as Fletcher's House.

SAINT
ANTHONY'S

JOHN
ALLSUP

This, it is believed, stands on the site of the old Vicarage in which John Fletcher, the Elizabethan dramatist and collaborator with Beaumont, was born in 1579. The house was either wholly or partly rebuilt early in the eighteenth century but it is certainly still in a wonderfully good state of preservation with some beautiful, half-timbered oak rooms. John was the second son of Richard Fletcher, Vicar of Rye, who was subsequently Dean of Peterborough, Bishop of Bristol and Worcester and finally of London. He is also remembered by the fact that he was at Fotheringay when poor Mary, Queen of Scots, was executed and gave justifiable offence to her friends by greeting the executioner's gesture of holding up the bloody head with the words, "So let Queen Elizabeth's enemies perish." A curious example of Christian charity!

Nevertheless, Fletcher's House is worth a visit. The next building on the corner of Lion Street and Church Square is an attractive shop called The Merrythought.

We will explore the Church on another journey so turn sharp right now into Church Square along the path with a few attractive houses on our right. The building with a crooked chimney, on the corner in front of you, is the Old Customs House, once known as Grene Hall. Queen Elizabeth I is said to have been entertained here when she came in 1573. Notice the door at the foot of the chimney stack which must surely be the entrance to a mighty cellar.

Now, with the churchyard wall on your left, walk up the west side of Church Square with a few agreeable Georgian houses on your right, until you come to another of Rye's showpieces. This fifteenth century half-timbered house is called St. Anthony's and has been cleverly restored. At one time the corner portion was a grocer's shop.

We are now at the corner of what I believe to be the most beautiful street in England. There are three superb streets in Rye - Market Street only a few hundred yards from where we stand, is wide and bright and dominated by the Town Hall. Mermaid Street which we have not yet visited, is the most famous, the most photographed and the most sketched. But Mermaid Street, with all its notoriety, sometimes gives the impression of being chilly and sunless - and when the tourists have gone, almost lonely.

Not so, the beautiful street on our right with the melodious name of Watchbell Street. Again, every building has obviously been cared for and cherished, and each seems to be a contrast to its neighbour. In summer it almost basks without being complacent. In winter it is serene because there is no way through for traffic and those who are fortunate to live in it, move quietly over its cobbles. And throughout the year, unless it is foggy, the view to the south and west from its abrupt ending is superb.

The street is named after the alarm bell used to warn the citizens that once again the French had been sighted in the Channel. It is easy to imagine how it would ring out across the huddled streets and round the church in time of danger and it saw plenty of that. Almost every building hereabouts was probably destroyed by fire during the great French raid in 1377.

Watchbell Street starts where we are standing. Its continuation to our left as far as the restored Methodist Church is part of Church Square and is so named but we might turn that way first and wander back down its whole length. All the houses, except perhaps the old red-brick Police Station, are worthy of notice but two are of particular historical significance although both have been partially restored. The first is surprisingly named 'Friars of the Sack'. The ancient walls must have withstood the great fire of the French raid. It was built in 1263 by a community of Friars who obviously wore sackcloth! Its gable-end faces the churchyard and the Gothic doorway is below the level of the pavement. Stand back to notice a large traceried window above. This little community and the Friary was dissolved in 1307 but the name lives on as you will see recorded on the pottery plaque designed by local craftsmen.

WATCHBELL STREET

Close by is a narrow alley marked Hucksteps Row, burrowing between and under overhanging houses and surely leading between the gardens of the old houses to the edge of the cliff. The entrance is clearly marked 'Private'. And before we express indignation, let us remember that all these houses are in private ownership and are kept in immaculate condition by citizens of Rye who often, in the summer months, must weary of being stared at through their windows so close to the pavements.

A little further along is another ancient building called the 'Old Store House', set well back from the street. This was undoubtedly part of the nearby Friary, although the original buildings which stood between the two, were probably destroyed by the French. There is an inscription on the wall which announces: *Restored 1898*.

Walk back now towards the view at the end of the street. It does not matter on which side you stroll. If you visit it first in spring or early summer you will be cheered by wisteria against white walls. There will be flowers behind windows and the gleam of brass knockers. On one side you may be surprised to see some dignified offices of professional gentlemen and again you will realize how typical of Rye is this street, because there are no great houses built by the wealthy. Everywhere is evidence of respect for the past and appreciation of so peaceful a haven in which to live. There are no shops in Watchbell Street and fortunately very little wheeled traffic because there is no through road when it reaches the edge of the cliff at the west end.

Halfway along the street on the left is the Roman Catholic Church dedicated to St. Anthony of Padua. This beautiful building is just seventy years old and is in startling contrast to every other building in the street - or indeed in Rye. The style is 'Spanish Roman' and it has been well described as a miniature basilica. The marble altar is magnificent and the six bronze candlesticks were specially made for it by Florentine craftsmen.

A little further down the other side of the street is a narrow turning between the houses. This is Watchbell Lane which, after a few yards, turns sharply left and leads us on to a grassy level known as The Green. Vidler suggests that this footpath is where the alarm bell was placed but it is difficult to see why. Possibly on the Green itself but surely the more obvious position would be in the Lookout at the very end of the street, poised on the edge of the west cliff? This little terrace is now paved, fenced and furnished with a seat and we can realize at once how well placed a watchman would be on guard here.

To me, this is the most unforgettable corner of Rye. Behind us is the placid, cobbled street and on our right, the striking facade of the Hope Anchor Hotel which dominates this side of the town. Whether or not there was always an inn on this site the historians do not tell us but there is no doubt that at one time it was much used by smugglers and seamen. Directly below it, at the foot of the cliff, was the busiest part of Rye - the Strand with its bustling wharves and the Strand Gate at the bottom of Mermaid Street. There were commodious cellars too below the hotel, although these are now bricked up. It has always been believed that a secret passage, or steps, led from these right down through the cliff to the Strand below. More likely, I believe that there was a tunnel wide enough for a keg of brandy to be hauled up and a bale of Romney Marsh wool let down. The superb situation of this delightful inn suggests that it may well have been used by a more aristocratic company than patronised the Mermaid, only a few hundred yards away.

From the steps and front windows of the Hope Anchor and, from the Lookout, the prospect is unforgettable. Below is the Strand and the roofs of old warehouses, a glimpse of the Ship Inn and, the masts of shipping at the Quay just beyond. The river we see is the Tillingham as it joins the Brede, before the two rivers unite in Rock Channel with the Rother, almost under the Gungarden.

Camber Castle is not always easy to see although it is almost straight in front of us. 'Natural camouflage helps to merge it into the surrounding marsh and it is difficult to realize that it was built on a spit of shingle only just above the level of the gradually receding sea. The view further to the west is becoming familiar. Winchelsea on its wooded hill, originally with the shape of the old black windmill without sails, silhouetted against the skyline. The latter was acquired by the National Trust but was destroyed in a fierce storm on 16th October 1987 before it could be restored. The further background is the Hastings Firehills and the tower of Fairlight Church.

This has been quite a long tour so we will save Trader's Passage and Mermaid Street for another journey. The quickest way back to the car may be to go down the steep Green Steps to the Strand. And even if you have explored the interior of the Hope Anchor you could pause at the Ship when you are safely down.

The Third Journey

These different approaches to the town have always been a source of anticipatory delight to me. This may be because I know that I shall never be disappointed at journey's end and that both distant and nearer views of Rye on its rocky pyramid are always dramatic. Even the last journey across the Marsh was unique, if not particularly beautiful, but from north and west the countryside is superb at all seasons.

This approach is from the west. We start at Hastings along the A259 Folkestone Road which leaves the promenade at the Old Fishmarket under the East Cliff and turns abruptly north through the outskirts of the picturesque Old Town. You may be tempted to leave the car for a few minutes to stroll over the shingle, between the black wooden sheds used for drying the fishing nets. There are many more fishing boats using Hastings than you will see at Rye but when not at sea these must be hauled up the beach because there is no harbour now. If you like fresh fish, here is a good place to buy it.

Hastings Old Town deserves a day to itself and will be mentioned later. As you drive on you will notice that the road is in a valley between the East and West Hills - the latter crowned by the spectacular ruins of William the Conqueror's castle and, honeycombed by the famous St. Clement's Caves.

So the road, well signposted, climbs up to the unattractive suburb of Ore and after forking right gives us a sudden, spectacular view to the north. The distant heights across the valley are wooded and, although we cannot see the little river in the valley, it is the Brede. Below you are the roofs of the growing village of Westfield but, regrettably out of sight, the little railway line from Hastings to Ashford passes through two almost secret 'Halts', delightfully named Three Oaks and Doleham, on its way to Winchelsea, Rye, Appledore and Ham Street. All the country you can see from this vantage point is worth exploring - preferably on foot from one of the Halts.

But we must be on our way. On the right, although we cannot yet see them, are the Fairlight Hills - the highest point of which is known as North Seat. From here it is sometimes possible to see the coast of France. A few hundred yards further on is the roadside sign announcing Guestling at the brow of the formidable White Hart Hill which, at the beginning of the century, must have been a fearful obstacle for horse-drawn traffic. On the right is a road signposted to Pett, which would take us eventually down to the coast or up to Fairlight church. But the A259 drops sharply as soon as it has passed the White Hart Inn. Here it is dangerous for the driver to take his eye off this curving road but as the descent begins, the first glimpse of Rye Bay can be seen to the south-east, straight ahead. A few minutes ago we were in a town but if the day is clear, this sudden panoramic vista of sea and the distant coastline is dramatic. About halfway down the hill on our side is a lay-by in which it is worth stopping for a few minutes. Glancing back to our right, is the now familiar silhouette of Fairlight Church on the skyline and further east the sharp, narrow spire of Pett Church which is more than a mile from the sea.

At the foot of the hill there is not much to see of the village of Guestling. A delightful but lonely little church is well off to the right but not visible from our main road which curves tantalizingly now through pleasant, rural country. The next hamlet, which is little more than a row of weather-boarded cottages on our left, is delightfully named Guestling Thorn. Why, I do not know, but not so many years ago one of the cottages adjoined a working forge. Several tempting little lanes leave the A259 on the north side of the road and plunge down into the Brede valley towards farms and cottages near Three Oaks and Doleham in the heart of the country we glimpsed from the outskirts of Ore. Every mile of this stretch of rural Sussex is worth exploring on foot. In spring the hedgerows of the deep, narrow lanes gleam with primroses and later in the year with pink campions and cow parsley.

Icklesham, the next village, is long and straggling with some modern development but more open farmland on the seaward side. This corner of Sussex seems to specialize in soft fruit. The most interesting part of Icklesham is at the eastern end where there is an Oast House, an old inn just off the main road and a beautiful little Norman church on the other side. Once through the village the road sweeps down towards the marshlands which surround Winchelsea. Again - and much nearer now - the best view yet of Rye. The Brede valley is on the left and on the northern skyline is the Udimore ridge, along which we shall travel on our next journey. Towards the foot of the hill, where we are warned to *Reduce Speed Now*, we have a good glimpse of Winchelsea on its wooded hill.

Now is the moment of decision. You may, if you wish, bypass Winchelsea and hurry on to Rye. This would be a mistake. Winchelsea is Rye's sister 'Antient Town'. Once she was bigger and more important than Rye and, although I shall give more space to this my home town *[Ed. 1971-81]* later, I suggest that if you have half-an-hour to escape from the everyday world, you enjoy now your first visit to this astonishing and beautiful backwater. Over fifty years ago, E. V. Lucas described Winchelsea thus - "Since there is no other town throned like this upon a green hill to be gained only by massive gateways." This is still so, although from this approach we miss one of the three gates which is about half a mile distant, still standing lonely and defiant at the bend in a leafy lane leading to Pett. In a different way Winchelsea is as unique as Rye with which it has always been closely associated. We visit this superb relic of a glorious past with more time to spare in the next chapter but if this is your first sight of it you will not regret leaving the A259 at a sharp bend at the top of the hill which is clearly signposted 'Winchelsea Town'. Just before turning left into a broad road lined with trees you will see the ruins of an ancient stone building in the field on the right. This is all that remains of St. John's Hospital. After the turn you are on the old Folkestone road through Winchelsea. Drive slowly. On the right, between the trees is a fine house in Tudor style, known as Greyfriars, in the grounds of which are the ruins of one of Winchelsea's ancient priories. Next on the right, in the centre of its great churchyard in the heart of the town, is the magnificent church which is visited by thousands of tourists each year. Leave the car somewhere hereabouts - there is no public car park yet in Winchelsea - stroll down the main street towards the great Strand Gate and the Lookout. It is rumoured that not so many years ago, a citizen of Winchelsea was paid a small annual fee to go here daily to make sure that the French were not coming! When this ancient custom was instituted, they often were. Pause on the raised pavement and look through the arch to see Rye framed like a perfect picture between the great stone walls of the ancient gateway. The view from the Lookout across the flat marshland to the caravan camp at Winchelsea Beach shows clearly that the sea reached the base of the cliff on which we are now standing. Away to the left is our first glimpse on this approach to Rye of the squat shape of Camber Castle and beyond is the mouth of the Rother and the gleam of Camber Sands on the other side of the estuary. On the horizon, more to the south if it is clear enough, is the outline of the Nuclear Power Station of Dungeness looking like a great battleship. The canal below us, not far from the base of the cliff, is the young Military Canal which ends near Pett Level after running inland from Hythe as a defence against a Napoleonic invasion.

But that is enough. You will return. Back to the car and under the great arch, down the steep hill to Winchelsea's old strand. Sharp right on to the A259, over the River Brede and then along the straight Military Road across the sheep dotted Marsh to the outskirts of Rye. Take a road on the right signposted Rye Harbour, cross the Brede again and pull into a lay-by on the left. From here is yet another wonderful view of the town much appreciated by artists. Now we are looking from below to the south frontage of the town dominated by the facade of the Hope Anchor. The houses and the green cupola of the Franciscan church in Watchbell Street are seen from a different angle and, as always, the tower of the Parish Church with its gilded weathercock - which is not a cock - crowns the pyramid.

There is no need to go on to Rye Harbour now. Go back to the main road, which swings round sharply to the right over another bridge, with a sluice which controls the placid waters of the little

Tillingham just before it joins the Brede, almost opposite the lay-by where we paused just now. There is a car park here. Turn right again where once large timber yards stood on each side of the road. This is the Strand which was the most important trading area of the medieval town, although today most of the old timber warehouses have been converted to shops and the land nearby redeveloped as retirement flats. The modern Heritage Centre with its superb Town Model exhibition now stands on this reclaimed industrial area. This fascinating corner of Rye was, of course, outside the walls and until the end of the last century there were two shipbuilding yards here.

The most important street in Tudor times was undoubtedly Mermaid Street and it is still the best-known thoroughfare in Rye. It is probably the most photographed and most sketched street in Britain and when you stand at its foot and look up its cobbled slopes you will understand why. Somewhere near its junction with three other narrow streets was the Strand Gate and, if you look carefully you will see a wall plaque, the legend on which reads:

Near this spot formerly stood the Strand Gate. This was part of the defences erected in 1329. This gate and the Postern Gate at the foot of Conduit Hill were destroyed in the late 18th century. The stone with the Borough Arms carved on it on the wall above was over the centre of the arch of the Strand Gate.

I have always thought it better to walk up Mermaid Street for the first time rather than explore it from the top but the best approach is a matter of opinion. Mermaid Street is still incomparable and you must savour it slowly, remembering that this was the entry to the town of all visitors who came to Rye by sea. Your first impressions of its character and architecture are not likely to be the same as those who came here in the busy Elizabethan times. Most of the houses date from the fifteenth to seventeenth centuries but again, the appeal of this street to a modern visitor is the astonishing variety of the buildings and the care with which they are cherished today.

Before you take your first step on to the cobbles, look to the right and try to picture what the building on the corner was like when it was a notorious haunt of smugglers called The London Trader Inn (now The Borough Arms). This is hardly surprising because it is close to the quay.

So take Mermaid Street gently. Do not be too influenced by Guide Books or what is written here. We can give you nothing more than a background although it is one of the most written-about streets in England and some visitors will have travelled halfway round the world to stand here.

On your right, after a few steps, is the foot of Trader's Passage. We saw the top of this on the Green outside the Hope Anchor. The prospect up this narrow cobbled way is enchanting. A 'trader', of course, is another name for a smuggler.

The first building on the right is fifteenth century. It is now a private house but one of Rye's Guide Books says that there are frescoes on the staircase which are over 400 years old. The next two houses on this side of the street are named Elders House and Quaker House, which are self-explanatory. Opposite the latter is the magnificent Hartshorn House, formerly known as the Old Hospital because it was used as a hospital during the Napoleonic wars. This, with its three overhanging gables, is now undoubtedly the finest house in the street. It was built in the fifteenth century and reconstructed about 100 years later. Once it was the home of Samuel Jeake II whose property it became when he married Elizabeth Hartshorn. This member of the Jeake family, as we have already read, was a member of one of Rye's most famous families of merchants. Opposite is Jeake's Storehouse and if you look carefully you will see two small plaques set in the wall. Both have Latin inscriptions, one of which may be translated as 'the

MERMAID
STREET

JOHN
ALLSUP

foundation of this house was laid at noon on June 13th, 1689.' It was first used for storing wool.

Jeake's Storehouse, like Lamb House which we shall visit shortly, has considerable literary associations. At the beginning of this century it was the home of the American author and poet Conrad Aiken. Margaret Brentnall in her book, *The Cinque Ports*, tells us that it became the meeting place of many writers and artists including T. S. Eliot, Julian Huxley, Dame Laura Knight and Paul Nash who, of course, lived only a few hundred yards away at the top of East Street.

The next house on the right is called Robin Hill and is also privately owned. It is said to be rich in oak beams and chimney-corners and boasts one of the finest timbered and straw plastered bedrooms in existence today.

And now we come, on the opposite side of the street, to the really world-famous Mermaid Inn. The reader must form his own opinion of this renowned tourist attraction, which was founded in the eleventh century and rebuilt in 1420. There is no question that this was the centre of the smuggling activities of Rye. And little wonder, for it is barely 300 yards from the Strand, which once was the busiest part of the town. The most notorious of all the smugglers in the south of England, known as the Hawkhurst Gang, made their headquarters here and brazenly slaked their thirst for all to see. No doubt they had plenty of friends in Rye who would give them quick warning if the Revenue men dared to show themselves in the town.

It is difficult to imagine as we stand outside this ancient tavern that in Tudor and Jacobean days this quiet street was the centre of the town's life and was once called Middle Street. All the houses we have seen must have belonged to influential and proud families whose fortunes were made by trading, not all of which may have been legal.

But the Mermaid is unique and some fascinating details of some of the Corporation's celebrations there are given in Geoffrey Bagley's, *Old Inns and Ale-Houses of Rye*. Apart from the smuggling stories associated with it, the Mermaid has always had an important part to play in the town's history. It made history again in 1973 when, on the last day of October, the late sixteenth Duke of Norfolk, Lord Lieutenant of Sussex and Earl Marshal of England, presented the Queen's Award to Industry to Michael Gregory, then owner of the hotel. The award was made "for its contributions to the export industry." In the year ending September 1972, the hotel attracted 3,345 overseas visitors who spent £67,000 which was 42% of the hotel's business.

The arrival of the Duke at 1 p.m. was preceded in the morning by some typical Rye business. Perce Sherwood, who was not only the town crier but also town sergeant, custodian of the Town Hall, chief mace bearer and once the late night porter of the Mermaid, toured the streets with his crier's bell and announced the Duke's imminent arrival!

Architecturally, the Mermaid is more impressive from the rear. The street perhaps is too narrow to appreciate the gabled frontage, which has been restored. The present building is believed to be late fifteenth century but there is a much older barrel-vaulted cellar under the hall. One of the many showpieces is a magnificent fireplace (12½ feet wide x 4½ feet deep) in the bar, in which in winter, great logs of Sussex oak keep out the cold. The main door is on the right of the covered way, which leads to a spacious yard at the rear, where there is another entrance to the hotel. Here there could have been stables and from the yard, a narrow cobbled lane leads down to the part of the High Street known as The Mint. The interior of the hotel is fascinating - a maze of twisting passages, dim staircases, unexpected steps and a wealth of dark oak beams and panelling but now well lit and warmed and worthy of its accolade.

[Ed. Over the past 25 years the Hotel has changed hands but continues to provide service to the thousands of tourists who visit Rye each year. It has a reputation for good food and hospitality and has recently opened a function suite which retains the old features of the hotel building in a pleasant mix of modern comfort.]

When you can desert the Mermaid it is only a few steps to the top of the street where it joins West Street. Turn right, and on your right is Rye's biggest and most important mansion, known as Lamb House. We have already been reminded that several generations of Rye's famous family lived here and that George I was entertained in the house soon after it was rebuilt by James Lamb, in about 1722. It was badly damaged by bombs in 1940 and sadly the famous Garden Room was completely destroyed. It was in this delightful retreat that Henry James, the famous American author, wrote some of his later books. He loved Rye and lived here from 1897 until 1916 as is recorded on a wall plaque. Those pre-war days must have been a wonderful period in the cultural history of Rye which has always had an attraction for writers, poets and artists. We are told that many literary celebrities such as Wells, Chesterton and Belloc visited James here. After the latter's death the house was let to two of the Benson brothers. Novelist E. F. Benson, who was Mayor of Rye for three successive years and who was given an Honorary Freedom of the Borough, lived here until 1940. Eight years later the James family - still the owners - presented the house to the National Trust who repaired it skilfully and set aside one small room in memory of Henry James. This room and the superb garden are open to visits on Wednesday and Saturday afternoons from Easter to October. The house is privately occupied and its literary tradition was enhanced most recently in the 1970s by the tenancy of the distinguished author Rumer Godden.

Turn left at the top of West Street into the north side of the delightful Church Square, passing on the way the "House with the

LION
STREET

John
Allsup

Crooked Chimney" which we first saw when we approached from the other direction.

Now is the time to visit the Parish Church of St. Mary. You can indeed walk right round it first and, during the summer months, can climb to the top of the tower for a magnificent view of the surrounding country. You may be glad to pause for breath on the first landing to inspect the mechanism of the oldest working church clock in the country which is reputed to have been made by a craftsman of Winchelsea in 1515.

There are eight bells in the belfry and I never sidle past them without remembering the late Dorothy Sayers' superb story, *The Nine Tailors*.

The best view - indeed the only possible vantage point - from which to see the famous clock face above the great north door, is from Lion Street at its junction with Market Street. This prospect is probably photographed as often as Mermaid Street. The main attraction is the pair of cherubic Quarter Boys - one on each side above the beautiful clock face - who may be seen to strike the quarters but not the hours. These boys are fibreglass replicas of the originals which have been carefully restored and are now safe from wind and rain in the Chapel of St. Clare, inside the church. Note also the grim inscription between the boys. The quotation, from the Apocrypha reminds us that: *For our time is a very shadow that passeth away.*

To some people a church is little more than a historic monument. To others it is first a place of worship and there is no doubt that St. Mary the Virgin has been that for more than 800 years. It is still the very heart of our town, justly and typically crowning the hill on which Rye has risen above the sea. It has played its part in history. It has been called the Cathedral of East Sussex but I can never think of it as such for it seems to me to belong exclusively to Rye. It was looted and burned by the French invaders in 1377. Its bells were taken triumphantly to France and recovered soon after by the valiant men of Rye and Winchelsea. In the last war it was damaged by bomb blast. It has suffered and recovered with its people and it still serves them.

In the church you may buy an excellent Official Guide illustrated with colour photographs. Both the Town Guides also contain distinguished and scholarly reference to its history, its architecture and ornaments. All, or any of these handy guides, are easier to take round than this book, which I hope will serve as a reminder of what you have appreciated. I suggest that you make sure of seeing the following: the great 18 ft pendulum of the clock swinging with dignity above the north transept just inside the door; the Chapel of St. Clare with the original Quarter Boys on the north wall and the magnificent mahogany Altar Table; the Burne-Jones window dedicated to the memory of Mary Tiltman in the north aisle; the Norman sedilia in the south transept and above it the magnificent 1928 window in memory of A. C. Benson, Master of Magdalene College, Cambridge, and author of the words of *Land of Hope and Glory.*

When you are ready to go - and hopefully have left your offering to help to preserve this great and noble church - leave by the north door and follow the path into the churchyard.

The churchyard is large and, not surprisingly, is reputed to be haunted by the ghost of the unfortunate Allen Grebell who was murdered here by the 'sanguinary butcher' called Breads. Incidentally, a replica of the latter's skull may be seen in the Heritage Centre and a memorial tablet to his victim, the Mayor, in the Chapel of St. Clare.

Enough is enough. The Strand, Mermaid Street, Lamb House and the Church will bring you many memories, so back to the car along Watchbell Street, stopping at the Hope Anchor for refreshment if you wish. Notice that just beyond the Green at the top of Trader's Passage on the town side, is a small walled rose garden with a lawn in the centre. Round the walls are some tombstones. Is this, I wonder, the burial ground of the Quakers or other Nonconformists who had a chapel off Mermaid Street?

Take Trader's Passage slowly. It is a gem set in this most beautiful corner of Rye and takes you back down to the Oak House at the foot of Mermaid Street.

The Fourth Journey

The last of our suggested approaches to Rye is from Battle, through which delightful town runs the A2100, which leaves the main London-Hastings road (A21) at John's Cross a mile or so south of Robertsbridge. I believe I have left the most intriguing route to the last. They have all meant much to me across the years but this particular way is still rural, well wooded and a road for all seasons.

Coming from the north into Battle, our inconspicuous way out of the town - almost before we've had time to see it - is a sharp, narrow turning on the left. This road is easy to miss because it is not obviously signposted and its name, on the right-hand side just past a small greengrocer's shop on the corner, is difficult to see. It is Mount Street and if you wish to see Battle before you go on to Rye there is an entrance to a car park a few yards along on the right.

Mount Street soon gives place to Caldbec Hill and within a few minutes we are in delightful country. The road is narrow and winding and soon drops sharply to a bridge over the mainline railway to Hastings, then up to the hamlet of Whatlington. There is nothing much to see here where we join the A21 for about a mile before turning right off the main road where Rye (11½ miles) is signposted for the first time. Our new road is the B2089 and, just past a fork in the road, it is worth pulling up to enjoy the view of rolling woodlands to the north and a superb vista to the south. The woods through which our road winds belong to the Forestry Commission, with discreet parking and picnic sites. The road dips between some magnificent beeches and then takes us on towards the oddly named Cripps Corner which is not much more than a pub on one side of the road and a garage on the other. Before reaching the crossroads, a bridge takes us over the A229 from Maidstone to Hastings. Once over the tricky crossing there is a fine wood of conifers on the right *[Ed. destroyed in 1987 storms]* which always reminds me of the pine woods I have seen in Austria and the Dolomites - woods through which wolves might prowl in less civilized surroundings! At most times of the year you may well see and hear foresters at work in the woods through which our road passes for two or three miles. These woods are marked on the Ordnance Survey Map (Sheet 199) as Brede High Wood and are the property of Southern Water. Nevertheless, there is at least one public footpath marked on the south side of the road and room to park a car. It is possible to walk right through these woods but it is difficult to find the large Powdermill Reservoir which supplies Hastings with water, for it is well hidden amongst the trees. The narrow lanes meandering through all this country between the villages of Sedlescombe and Brede are worth exploring - particularly in the spring.

The next hamlet on our way to Rye is Broad Oak where our road crosses the A28 to Hastings. There are several 'Broad Oaks' in Sussex so this one is sensibly known as Broad Oak Brede.

Rye is almost in sight now as our road rises between Broadland Wood on the way to Udimore. This ridge divides the valleys of two of Rye's rivers - to the north the little Tillingham and to the south the bigger Brede. It is farming country with fruit trees on the sunny slopes and, of course, hundreds of sheep on the levels below. Before we reach the outskirts of straggling Udimore there is a hilly lane on the right which leads, eventually, back to the village of

Brede. It also leads to Brede Place, a fourteenth century manor-house in which Clare Sheridan, the sculptress, lived from 1936-47.

Udimore's church is a few hundred yards off the road but there are no other noteworthy buildings in the village, except the magnificent farmhouse called Knellstone, dating from the early seventeenth century. The lane leading to it is signposted. Soon after passing through another wood the country opens out on each side of the road. To the north, across the wide valley of the Tillingham, more trees are hiding Rye Foreign and, to the south, the valley of the Brede, with a fine glimpse of Winchelsea on its tree-clad hill. Soon you will see a narrow lane on the right. It is not signposted but is known locally as Dumb Woman's Lane and leads steeply down to the marsh and to Winchelsea Railway Station which is at least a mile from Rye's sister 'Ancient Town.' A little further on we get our first glimpse of the sea since leaving Battle and then, just before the road drops to Rye, we see the Town Sign on the left. There is nothing of special architectural interest here as we coast down Cadborough Hill, now known as Udimore Road. Historically, we might remember that it was below the Cadborough Cliffs on the south side that Rye, in the last war, placed anti-aircraft guns which faced the English Channel. Always Rye's defences have challenged any enemy who crossed the sea.

Cadborough Hill leads us into Ferry Road, we cross the Tillingham and are in Rye again, over the railway crossing and into a big car park at the railway station.

Most of the town has been explored during the first three journeys but what I now suggest will leave you time to go back to what you might like to see again. So turn up Ferry Road to its junction with busy Cinque Ports Street, cross over and take your choice of right or left. If you choose the latter you need only walk a few yards to see the entrance of a narrow alley leading up to the Mint through a gap in the Town Wall which, you will remember, ran along the south side of Cinque Ports Street. This passage is known traditionally as The Needles although nobody seems to know why. Perhaps because it threads a tortuous way up to the Mint at the side of the Standard Inn? You will remember that the Mint is a curving continuation of High Street and a most attractive part of Rye. It should not be hurried. Records of the Standard exist since 1866 but the original must be older than that because it is not many steps down from the site of the old Strand Gate and would have been well patronized by sailors and fishermen. A little further up the street, on the same side, is another inn - the Old Bell - which must have been equally popular and in fact it still is. Tradition suggests that it was frequented by smugglers in the seventeenth century. Almost opposite this inn a narrow, cobbled lane leads up to the back of the Mermaid Inn. This, and another cul-de-sac which joins it at its foot, is most attractive. We have not much information about Rye's Mint or exactly where it was. Vidler tells us that coins of King Stephen were issued from the town in 1141 and that "the Mint probably remained open until the accession of Henry II."

The pleasant houses on the left, at the foot of the narrow street, are modern. They are set well back and have obviously taken the place of some older, crowded dwellings, probably like those opposite, which still seem to be supporting each other. Notice David Sharp's main Pottery at the foot of the street and then we are back at the site of the old Strand Gate.

Should you prefer to turn right at the junction of Ferry Road with Cinque Ports Street you will reach the same place more quickly. Cross the road and you are in the district known as The Wish. This is the area which lay outside the town wall, but you may see part of this if you take the short street opposite the Pipemakers Arms, known as Wish Ward. The wall, in fine preservation, is easy to see on the left together with an old well, brick cistern and pump.

Back at the site of the Strand Gate at the bottom of Mermaid Street you may be tempted to explore this again or to go up Trader's Passage to Watchbell Street.

From below here, you also have the opportunity to stroll east, past a pleasant row of town houses opposite the Ship Inn. These are not incongruous and are a credit to the town and their architect. Still walking east you come to South Undercliff where the workmen's houses, built in the last century with slate roofs, are not so felicitous. The road swings sharply to the left and you are now under the Gungarden and will notice the steep flight of steps leading down from the Ypres Castle Inn. Opposite is a rough road leading to the riverbank and, by turning left, you can walk along to the Fishmarket and the Town Salts, with a splendid close view of the fishing boats either moored or coming up with the tide. From here also you can admire the backs of the houses perched at the edge of the cliff at the top of East Street where it joins Market Street. The Town Salts and the river here are not particularly beautiful but there is always something going on.

But whether you come down the Wish or the Mint you may prefer to explore the Strand and the Quay. This area was once dominated by the unusual and enormous timber-built warehouses although most have long since been converted for other commercial and domestic uses. Ships were still being built in this part of Rye at the end of the last century and there were yards on each side of the river. Even up until a few years ago, ships carrying timber came up the river as far as this quay and unloaded their cargoes which were stored nearby.

I am very fond of this corner of Rye, just outside the town walls. Pirates, smugglers, sailors from many lands, merchants, honest citizens, ship builders and Huguenot craftsmen all gathered here just outside the Strand Gate. Perhaps their ghosts still walk on moonlit nights when traffic on the A259, which circles the town, is stilled. When you have explored the narrow ways between the warehouses and the Ship - if indeed you are able to pick your way between the parked cars - cross the road and see what little boats are moored at the Quay. The big sluice gate on your right controls the water of the Tillingham and holds back the tide coming up Rock Channel. Beyond, on the other side of the main road, is the gaunt windmill without sails which you will have seen as soon as you stepped clear of the warehouses. You may have had your first glimpse of this when you came down Ferry Road.

Rye can be very windswept and no doubt this was a good site for a windmill, placed conveniently close to the quay and the town. Its working days were over when it was destroyed by fire in the summer of 1930. It was apparently partially rebuilt but I am told that it was not possible to find a craftsman who could fit new sails. You can take a closer look by crossing the main road and taking the footpath on the town side of the river. Cross the railway line with care and the mill is on your right. If you wish, you may then follow the path along the river bank until it reaches Ferry Road, only a few yards from a car park.

If this is the last day of your first visit to Rye you can leave this book in the car and go your own way for yet another glimpse of what has pleased you most. You may want to visit the church again or wander up Watchbell Street and pause in the lookout to see the dusk come down. And don't forget another look at the Flushing Inn, the Mermaid and the Hope Anchor. If there is time you will not regret another visit to the Gungarden and the Ypres Tower. And of course there is Trader's Passage, the High Street gently curving into the Mint, and the little anonymous graveyard at the top of Trader's Passage. And always, throughout the seasons, there are the views of the Marsh and green levels between Rye and the Fairlight Hills to the south-west.

But you will cherish your own memories of this sturdy little town, which historically and physically, is unique in Britain.

You will come back again, and be welcome.

YPRES CASTLE

STEPS TO
THE
TOWN
SALTS

JOHN ALLSUP

88

Chapter Four:

Round and About

Rye is an admirable centre for the tourist. It is close to the sea and the wonderful sands of Camber and within comfortable petrol-saving reach of country, which as we have already seen, is rich in historical associations. It is on the edge of Kent with many beautiful, peaceful villages. There are ruins of mighty castles at Hastings, Bodiam and Pevensey, not forgetting the little fortress built by Henry VIII between Rye and Winchelsea, known as Camber Castle.

And then there is the Marsh, which is not really marshy but which provides the finest grazing for sheep in Britain and which we have already glimpsed from Rye and Winchelsea. There is nothing else quite like this 20 mile stretch of flat land reclaimed from the sea which is criss-crossed with dykes and ditches and protected now behind a strong sea wall. It has been called 'The Fifth Quarter of the Globe' but on today's maps you will see that it is divided by title into Guldeford Level to the east of Rye, then Walland Marsh in Kent, with Denge Marsh to the south of it and bounded by the great shingle bank of Dungeness jutting into the Channel. Further east, up to the line of old cliffs that run beyond Hythe and down to Dymchurch Wall on the south, is Romney Marsh itself.

You could spend many days exploring this little tract of land which is so unlike any other part of England. You will admire the clarity of the light and the purity of the air. You may discover beautiful little churches in lonely places. You may walk the banks of the Military Canal built as a defence against Napoleon. There are lapwings in their hundreds tumbling over the fields and rare wild flowers to be found on the shingle wastes between Lydd and Dungeness. The Marsh has its own literature. Kipling mentions Dymchurch in *Puck of Pook's Hill*. Russell Thorndyke gave us *Dr Syn*; William Cobbett in his *Rural Rides*, wrote admiringly of the road from Appledore to Old Romney and the Reverend Richard Barham (one-time Rector of Snargate) wrote *Ingoldsby Legends*. And today, Walter Murray's *Romney Marsh* has almost become a standard work.

The Marsh also has its own mystique. You will love it or hate it and I can do no more than introduce you to a fragment of it.

But to the north and west of Rye you will find undulating country, fertile valleys, glorious woodland and gentle streams. Spring comes early to the deep, sheltered lanes between Pett and Hastings and the gorse-clad Firehills high above the sea are a tonic throughout the year. For the walker and the naturalist this corner of Sussex is a delight.

A selection of such places follows in alphabetical order. Three Ordnance Survey Maps will help the explorer – Explorer Sheet 125: Romney Marsh; Landranger Sheet 189: Ashford and Romney Marsh; Landranger Sheet 199: Eastbourne and Hastings.

~~~~~~~~~

APPLEDORE is only six miles from Rye but is actually in Kent, in the north-west corner of the Marsh. It is an extremely attractive village with a broad main street, well-placed church and two pubs. It is at first difficult to realize that the sea is only nine miles away to the south and that once Appledore was proud of its shipyards on a river long since altered by a changing coastline. Some say that where the church now stands, once stood a castle built by the Danes in the reign of King Alfred. The castle was destroyed by the French during the fourteenth century but, long before that, the Romans tried landings here.

Although Appledore is the northern gateway to the Marsh, I am sure that its chief attraction is its position on the Royal Military Canal, along the side of which runs the road from Rye. This road is called the Military Road and leaves Rye at the foot of the A268 by which we entered the town on our first journey. It is a B road signposted 'Appledore', almost straight and completely level. On our left are the gentle cliffs that the tide once reached. On the opposite side of the road is the Rother which incorporates the canal until it reaches the second of two locks which is aptly named Iden Lock after the village of the same name on the heights above. The river here winds inland across the levels and the canal and road run straight and side by side and when both cross the Kent Ditch, we have left Sussex behind. This canal is peaceful and beautiful and for a few miles now is lined with elm trees. It is possible to walk along it and indeed, beyond Appledore, a section is in the care of the National Trust. On our left, soon we see the bluff cliff of the Isle of Oxney, of which more later. A narrow lane leads up to it just opposite Stone Bridge over the canal. A good place to stop for a picnic.

After enjoying Appledore you can explore much of the Marsh by leaving on the B2080 signposted 'New Romney'. A mile along this road you will pass Appledore Station on the Hastings-Ashford line. Once, from here, a branch line went on to Lydd and New Romney, with an extension to Dungeness but that is no longer open to passenger traffic.

BATTLE has already been mentioned in the last chapter but some further description may be helpful as it is only 14 miles from Rye and well worth a visit. It is a small, busy market town set in delightful country. The town is dominated by the great gateway of the Abbey built by William the Conqueror after winning the battle of Hastings about a mile to the south. The story of how the

Normans landed at Pevensey, marched to Hastings where they rested some days before riding on to meet the English at Telham, is told in the history books. Most of us have childhood memories of the story of how King`Harold and his sturdy Saxons fought and died that day. And when I go to Battle I am often reminded of a story, not so often told, of how a Norman troubadour named Taillefer opened the battle by riding alone towards the enemy, singing a song of heroes and tossing his lance into the air. Those who would read this story and a brief account of the battle will find it movingly retold by E. V. Lucas in his *Highways & Byways of Sussex*.

There is no doubt that the abbey was founded by William and the High Altar placed on the spot where Harold fell. The impressive gatehouse which we see today is fourteenth century and there is a fine fifteenth century house, which is now a café, in excellent preservation nearby. The abbot's house is now a private school but the grounds are maintained by English Heritage and are open during the season to visitors on payment of an entrance fee. There are several other interesting features in this compact and attractive little town, including a good bookshop.

BODIAM must not be missed. It is only 14 miles from Rye on the A268 through Peasmarsh and on through wooded country until it joins the A28 for a mile or two. The road now drops to the valley of the Rother, crossing first the single track of a disused railway which once ran from Headcorn Junction to Robertsbridge via Tenterden Town, and then over the river by a little hump-backed bridge. We are now in Kent and quickly through the hamlet of Newenden - remembering that this was once on navigable water - on the way to Sandhurst. Look for a turning on the left signposted 'Bodiam' and drop down again towards the Rother valley.

Opposite the Castle Inn is a good car park from which a path leads across a field to the most romantic and beautiful ruin in

Sussex. At all times of the year it is difficult not to be lyrical about this fairy-tale castle surrounded by a moat in which water-lilies flourish. Bodiam is serene and surprisingly isolated. Fortunately it is in the care of the National Trust so it is possible to buy a guide book at the small shop and there is also a little museum of finds made during restoration.

This castle is beautiful rather than historic. Nothing much except natural decay and skilled restoration has ever happened to it since its construction in the fourteenth century by Sir Edward Dalyngrige, a hero of Cressy and Poitiers. It must have been built on the banks of the river which at that time would have been very much wider and navigable to French raiders.

From the outside it looks almost untouched by time but the interior is dramatic. Don't miss the enormous castle well near the kitchen. Some historians have claimed that the great entrance gatehouse is possibly the most imposing in England and they could be right. Once seen, beautiful, lonely Bodiam can never be forgotten and I think that you will come back again.

BREDE, sitting on a hill above the river after which it is named, is a pleasant village. It is only about seven miles from Rye and could be visited on a trip to Hastings. Take the B2089 by way of Ferry Road, through Udimore to the Broad Oak crossroads, where you must turn sharp left downhill. The chief attraction of the village is a group of buildings round the church and pub opposite. There are several old tiled and timbered cottages and a village shop but the glory of Brede is its spacious church crowning the hill. There has been a sacred building here since about 1180 and obviously many changes have been made over the 800 years. Look for a fine pillar alms-box dated 1687 and, curiously enough, an elaborately carved Flemish oak chest which is claimed to be the cradle of Dean Swift! And do not miss the treasure from this century which is the

Virgin and Child carved from Sussex oak by Clare Sheridan in 1937. This famous sculptress lived for a time at Brede Place about a mile distant. Somehow it is seemly that this splendid house of God should be dedicated to St. George whose flag often flies proudly from its massive, square, embattled tower.

BROOKLAND is only six miles from Rye on Romney Marsh. Alphabetically, it is the first of several Marsh Churches which I shall mention, so here is the place to stress that a visitor to Rye should spend at least one day exploring the Marsh villages and particularly its churches. Most of these are remote from more than a few houses or a farm but this could be because some, like Old Romney, were once washed by tidal waters.

Brookland's church is now by-passed by the A259 and is literally unique because its bell tower stands in the churchyard and is not part of the main structure. No visitor who sees it for the first time can be surprised that it attracts tourists from all parts of Britain and many from overseas. Like most of the Marsh churches it was built on an artificial mound to raise it above the level of flood water. As it is in Kent - we shall have crossed the county boundary of the Kent Ditch on our way from Rye - it is fitting that it should be dedicated to St. Augustine, the first Archbishop of Canterbury. Nothing that I can say in this brief description of a beautiful and unusual church can be stated as well as has been done in the admirable Church Guide on sale in the church. It is written by Anne Roper, who is an acknowledged expert on Romney Marsh and its churches, and who writes of them with authority and affection. She believes that the present building was erected in the middle of the thirteenth century - probably on the site of an earlier Norman church.

The visitor, after entering by the north porch, will first be impressed by the size of the interior and then by its dignified simplicity. The box pews are in a remarkable state of preservation but the church has several special treasures. The first is the famous circular lead font. Miss Roper tells us that this is the most important of "the thirty lead fonts remaining in this country." Its workmanship - Norman or Flemish - is twelfth century. Note specially the ornamental arcading and signs of the Zodiac. It has been suggested that this treasure might have been stolen from a church in Normandy by some sailors from Rye and Winchelsea on a return 'raiding visit' to the French who so frequently attacked our two towns.

There is a fine reproduction of the Royal Arms over the south door but an even more exciting picture is the fragment of a wall painting in the south-east corner of the south aisle. This was uncovered during repairs in 1964 and shows the martyrdom of St. Thomas à Becket, Archbishop of Canterbury.

There is not much else of interest in the village which in the early nineteenth century was much used by smugglers. On one occasion in 1821 there was a particularly bloody battle between them and the 'Blockaders' who were led by three midshipmen. Four smugglers were killed and sixteen carried away wounded. Those who were captured were tried at the Old Bailey and this remote and unknown village in the mysterious Marsh achieved a brief notoriety.

Today, Brookland is almost surrounded by glasshouses and known for the propagation and sale of roses.

CAMBER, about four miles from Rye, is reached by a turning off the A259 on the right soon after leaving the town. A few yards away from this junction you will see the squat building of East Guldeford church. Although not classified as one of the group of Marsh churches, this one is on Guldeford Level in Sussex - not Kent. Like so many of these isolated churches this one is surprisingly large. There is nothing of particular interest inside except a three-decker pulpit and a medieval font of Purbeck marble. There are a few undistinguished wall paintings dating only from the last century. Actually the building is more impressive from the outside. There can be little doubt that this church was used by smugglers.

I mentioned in the description of the second approach to Rye that there was no need to linger in Camber. Not quite fair perhaps if you would like to enjoy the finest stretch of sand for bathing or walking along the Kent and Sussex coasts. No wonder that what was not so very long ago little more than a hamlet, is now a sizeable village with a large holiday camp and contemporary attractions for the visitor. In a fine summer, parents and children in search of sea, sun and sand will find Camber a delight. Approaching from Rye, visitors pass the famous links of the Rye Golf Club - one of the great seaside courses in the south of England.

CAMBER CASTLE is not at Camber but on the Winchelsea side of the Rother and has sometimes been called after Rye's sister town. You will never find it unless you are prepared to walk but it is certainly worth a visit. It has recently been placed under the guardianship of English Heritage who have made the ruins safe and now open the castle to visitors at weekends between July and September. The only way from Rye is by the Public Footpath (signposted Camber Castle) a few yards from the Rye Harbour road which leaves the A259 close by a garage and, almost immediately crosses the Brede. The path is along the riverbank for some distance and the castle is always in sight.

Curiously enough, in silhouette from a distance, it does not look like a ruin. Its outline of clover leaf design is still impressive.

Although it has no towers or battlemented gateways it looks like a castle and almost seems to be a natural part of a flat landscape. It is over fifty years ago that I first saw it as a child. As I was born in Hastings this must have been the second castle I had seen in my short life. Later, when I became a writer, I used it in a story for children which was set in Rye and which still sends readers to see it for themselves.

Camber Castle is believed to have been built by Henry VIII on a spit of gravel and the sea washed its walls. It was one of a series of gun forts which he built along the south coast as a defence against the French but it never fired a shot and, by the middle of the seventeenth century, the sea had receded leaving it marooned. Today, sheep graze peacefully round its sturdy walls.

DUNGENESS is almost literally out of this world - a steadily growing promontory of shingle jutting out into the Channel. It grows because the action of the tides, aided by the prevailing south westerly winds, carries the shingle down the coast and piles it up here. It is a stony desert but, paradoxically, naturalists find much to interest them in what growth there is of rare plants and vegetation. There are two lighthouses because the older, still standing, is no longer on the point of the promontory but at least one hundred yards inland from the slim newcomer which has taken its place. There is an important lifeboat station where the boat is launched down a steep slipway and, surprisingly, there is the terminus of the truly splendid Romney, Hythe and Dymchurch Railway which claims to be the smallest public railway in the world. The trains are hauled by steam locomotives which are replicas of famous railway engines. But overshadowing all is the great Nuclear Power Station which from a distance looks in silhouette like a monster battleship. Even the new lighthouse is dwarfed by the bulk of this silent, sinister giant, while the pylons striding inland across the flat landscape seem strangely out of place.

Some visitors are repelled by this vast expanse of shingle, seemingly so remote from civilization and normality but there are others who find solace in its solitude where the silence is broken only by the cries of wild birds. It is not surprising therefore that this stretch of coast is favoured by bird watchers - particularly those interested in migration. Dungeness also played a great part in the last war because it was from here that P.L.U.T.O. - Pipeline Under The Ocean - left the English shore for Calais. This was a well-kept secret because the pumps and machinery were hidden amongst fishermen's huts and evacuated bungalows.

The best way to reach Dungeness from Rye is to take the A259 across the Marsh and turn right on to the B2075 to Lydd, just before reaching New Romney. From the former, take another road signposted to the Nuclear Power Station and Dungeness. About a mile after leaving the town, you will see on the left a large mere - presumably flooded gravel pits - in which are several small islands which will probably be thick with birds. The village or hamlet of Dungeness is little more than a straggle of bungalows, fishermen's huts and two pubs. Our road is crossed by the tracks of the little railway - no gates or flashing lights - and then joins another road which runs right along the coast to New Romney, through Greatstone and Littlestone-on-Sea, both of which are popular holiday settlements with fine sands. From the road at Dungeness the sea is out of sight behind the piled shingle but if you walk across it you will see how the fishermen have to haul their boats up the steep bank. The sea is deep here and in bad weather large vessels are often able to anchor and shelter close to the shore. Large and varied catches of fish are made off Dungeness and sold to the discriminating natives and visitors.

FAIRFIELD is really nothing more than a farm and a church. But what a church! In some ways it is the gem of all the Marsh churches and stands in proud isolation about 200 yards off a minor road from Appledore, which joins the A259 at a sharp corner not far from Brookland. On the Ordnance Survey Map (Sheet 189) Fairfield church is only marked by a faint cross south of Beckett's Barn but the best way to reach it from Rye is along the A259. At a very sharp left-hand bend you will see, just off the road, a notorious smugglers' inn, aptly called the Woolpack, the name of which is painted on its roof. At the next corner, just ahead, take the narrow lane signposted 'Appledore'. There is nothing much to see except an expanse of flat marshland on each side of the road. However, soon after the second turning on the right signposted 'Snargate', you will see ahead the squat shape of Fairfield's church dedicated to St. Thomas à Becket and, curiously enough, the only Anglican church dedicated to the Archbishop and Martyr in this, his own diocese of Canterbury.

The only way to this isolated building is through a wicket gate and across a raised causeway. There is a small lay-by opposite this gate but the key to the church may be obtained from the farm on the opposite side of the road a little further on. It is usually to be found hanging beside the back door of the house.

The last time I visited Fairfield was on a weekday in February. No human being was in sight either on the road or in the farmhouse. As we closed the wicket gate to keep the sheep from straying on to the road, a cloud of lapwings rose from the other side of the dyke ahead. There were sheep and gulls everywhere and when we crossed the narrow bridge a pair of noble swans on the water regarded us without interest. From here it is obvious that the church was deliberately built on a mound to keep it above the flood waters of winter. Your first surprise will be that the walls are of brick. Your next surprise will be that the interior is bright, clean and tidy. What is more, it gives the impression that it is more than a museum and is really cared for as a quiet place of worship.

Like most of the Marsh churches an admirable Guide is available and from it you will learn that, early in the thirteenth century, it is recorded that the church "was built of materials which were easily expendable should the building cease to be required for worship." Presumably it was built of lath and plaster, with timber for the main structure. There is no doubt that the interior has been transformed several times during its 700 years of service. In 1912 the entire building was near collapse, so it was taken down and rebuilt using as much of the old material as possible - indeed some of the timbers are from the original building and are as sound as when they were first erected. The interior furnishings are eighteenth century - white box pews, large white three-decker pulpit and a tiny but beautiful altar which is, as it should be, the focal point of the building.

Like Rye's great church, I think this little lonely house of God has borne much witness and been visited by many from overseas. Fairfield is a good beginning to a tour of the Marsh churches, more of which will be mentioned in alphabetical order.

FAIRLIGHT and the **FIRE HILLS** are nearer Hastings than Rye but are certainly worth visiting if only as a change from the flat marshlands. A good approach would be to take the road signposted 'Winchelsea Beach' just before you reach the foot of Winchelsea's Strand Hill. This road passes through the modern settlement that has grown up round some caravan camps close to the beach and then, straight as a ruler, under the comparatively new sea wall with Pett Level on the right. Naturalists may wish to pause by the meres which are a haven for many birds. This part of the coast was considered very vulnerable during the last war and a constant watch was kept on it by night and day. As a precaution the marsh on the right was flooded. Before the wall was built, an old inn called The Ship stood in isolation until it was washed away in a great south-westerly gale. The cliff ahead is the easterly point of the Fairlight Hills and is called Cliff End. The hamlet at its foot is Pett Level. Just inland here the Royal Military Canal completes its journey from Hythe. Our road climbs steadily up to Fairlight church (540 feet above sea level), the tower of which we have often seen on the skyline from Rye and the surrounding country. In the summer months it is possible to climb the tower and enjoy magnificent views of Rye Bay and the undulating wooded land to the north. Soon after passing the church is a turning on the left leading to an ample parking space. The Fire Hills – so called because they blaze with gorse almost throughout the year – are now classified as a Country Park and are ideal for walking. The cliffs are high and dangerous here but the turf is soft, the air sweet and there is always something to see in the Channel. Hastings is out of sight to the west but Fairlight Cove and Ecclesbourne Glen are both within walking distance.

HASTINGS with its adjoining town of ST. LEONARD'S-ON-SEA now have a population of over 70,000 *[Ed. 1976]* and are still growing. We started our third journey to Rye from here but I make no apology for referring to it again because if you spared no more than a few minutes looking at 'The Old Town', you will not regret a second visit to the narrow streets, alleys and courts, crammed between the East and West Hills. From Fairlight, down through Ore to the beach where the fishing boats have been hauled up the shingle - not unlike those at Dungeness - will not take you more than fifteen minutes, and there are car parks on the beach itself. Forget the modern 'amusements' provided for the visitor and the sophistication of the other Hastings and the respectability of St. Leonard's to the west. Remember that where you are standing on the foreshore was one of the Cinque Ports and in the twelfth century supplied more ships to the King's Fleet than Winchelsea or

Rye. It was, of course, a navigable port then but the same series of storms which diverted the Rother from Old Romney and drowned Old Winchelsea in 1287, seems to have been responsible for the silting up of Hastings harbour. Although there were attempts to build a harbour arm to be connected to the mainline railway by a tunnel under Eastcliff these plans were abandoned.

In many ways Hastings Old Town is like Rye. It is full of surprises and fascinating little shops and pubs and the buildings are huddled companionably together. Two main streets, High Street with raised pavements, and All Saints Street run from the north down to the sea. Between them, where once ran a stream called the Bourne, is a comparatively new road which has relieved the other two of through traffic. The stream now runs underground. Terraces of attractive houses on each side of the steep valley look down on the roofs of the two main streets and are worth exploring. So are the three churches – St. Clements (1390) at the sea end and All Saints, and St. Mary, Star of the Sea at the north. See if you can find Tackleway and Tamarisk Steps and the way up to the East Hill from which you can look down on the beach and the famous black, tarred 'net shops' where the fishermen's nets are dried and mended.

But perhaps the West Hill crowned with the ruins of the Conqueror's Norman Castle will please you more. A lift from George Street, which leads from the East Parade to the foot of High Street, will save you a stiff walk. Apart from the castle, which is surprisingly large, the views out to sea and of the beach below are fascinating. The West Hill is well kept and attractive and a short stroll across the grass to the east will bring you to the entrance of St. Clement's Caves where there is a stimulating exhibition of smuggling activities on this coast. If you are not allergic to caves these are very fine specimens and well kept. They were probably once used by smugglers and during the last war were invaluable as Air-Raid Shelters.

IVYCHURCH is not much more than the splendid church of St. George with a friendly looking pub next door. If you find the Marsh churches fascinating, this is worth a visit and could be easily reached if you are making a tour from Fairfield and Snargate. If you are coming from Brookland continue east along the A259 and cross straight over Brenzett cross-roads onto a minor road past Brenzett Place. It is signposted "Ivychurch". My impressions of the church - of which I made a note on my last visit - may not be yours but I hope will persuade you to visit it. The building is surprisingly large and the sturdy tower, a Marsh landmark. Not surprisingly the fabric is very weather-beaten but was also damaged by flying bombs in the last war. Entrance is by the south porch, which is buttressed like a miniature castle but not until after my last visit did I read that there is a priest's chamber above the porch which would account for its size. No doubt this would also have been used by smugglers, as was a vault under the north aisle. Your first impression of the interior will probably be shock! *[Ed. 1976]* There are no pews or seats in the large nave. The floor and walls are clean but opposite the door against the north wall is what looks like a sentry box or road watchman's hut. Investigation proves this to be a "Hudd" which was moved to the graveside in Marsh winters to shelter the parson and keep his wig dry! In the chancel there are a few seats for today's small congregations. You will notice a splendid Royal Coat of Arms and some emblazoned text boards, which are typical of the Marsh churches. History relates that some of Cromwell's soldiers came this way and used the church as a dormitory for themselves and a stable for their horses.

LYDD is Romney's Corporate Member of the Cinque Ports and also has an enormous church. From Rye it can be reached from two directions - either from a turning on the right off the A259 just before it reaches New Romney or along the quieter road through

Camber. I like this self-contained and proud little borough which was almost certainly once on a wind-swept island between the Walland and Denge Marshes rather like an oasis. A tree-decked oasis too, which is a pleasant surprise. For many years Lydd has been remembered for its artillery ranges and military camp and now for its proximity to a small airport and the Nuclear Power Station. But today, more than ever, the pride and ornament of Lydd is the great thirteenth century Parish Church of All Saints on which all roads seem to converge. With justification this glorious building has been called "The Cathedral of the Marsh". The great tower was built by Thomas Wolsey who was rector of Lydd some years before he was made Cardinal. The money was raised from the prosperous wool merchants of those days. Not surprisingly, the top of this 132 ft. tower has often been used as a lookout and warning beacon - particularly at the time of the French raids because it was the custom of the Cinque Ports to try and warn each other of impending danger. But there was not much time between warning and attack in the last war for those on this part of the coast. In 1940 a bomb fell directly on the church, exploded on the high altar and completely destroyed the chancel. As if this was not enough, All Saints suffered further damage from flying bombs later. But the people of Lydd and their friends, although dismayed by the magnitude of their task, determined not only to repair their church but restore much of its original beauty. Look, for instance, in the Baptistry at the great stone walls from the original Saxon church and then at the ceiling of the new chancel.

NEW ROMNEY is only 13 miles from Rye and can be reached direct along the A259 to Folkestone or, if you are exploring the Marsh, approach along the B2070 from Ashford and Ivychurch. At first sight it is difficult to appreciate that this pleasant little town was once on the coast and one of the original Cinque Ports. Here too the wayward Rother once found the sea. From the wide High Street there is now no sign of the English Channel which is over one mile away at Littlestone. But like so many of the Marsh towns and villages, New Romney is dominated by its Parish Church. St. Nicholas is certainly worth seeing if only for its magnificent Norman Tower with its proud pinnacles and unusual west doorway sunk below the level of the pavement. On the coast road is a station, which is the headquarters of the Romney, Hythe and Dymchurch Light Railway. From here you can travel west to Dungeness or north-east to Dymchurch and Hythe. New Romney, which seems to have plenty of accommodation to offer, is an admirable centre from which to explore the Marsh and is within easy reach of Dymchurch, Hythe and Folkestone.

NORTHIAM is a large, attractive village only eight miles from Rye. Take the A268 up the hill to Playden and bear left through Peasmarsh, on to Four Oaks Corner, and then left on to the B2008 through Beckley, then right as signposted. This short journey is through pleasant, well-wooded country. Northiam has many interesting buildings but is mainly notable for two wonderful old houses and a village green with the remains of a great oak tree under which the first Queen Elizabeth dined on her way to Rye in 1573. The first of the two historic houses, known as Brickwall, is now a boys' school and just off the main road at the south end of the village. This is a magnificent specimen of a seventeenth century timber-framed house - certainly one of the best in the county. It photographs well from the splendid iron gates. Northiam's other fine mansion is Great Dixter about half a mile to the north. It is off the main road but is clearly signposted. This mansion, with a fine half-timbered front, dates from about 1450. It was restored in 1912 by Sir Edward Lutyens who also designed the superb topiary gardens which are now open to the public. Northiam's church is large and has a stone spire - unusual in Sussex - crowning a twelfth-fifteenth century tower. Inside, the font of Sussex marble is twelfth century. E. V. Lucas in his *Highways & Byways in Sussex* gives us a couplet used by the natives at the beginning of this century:

Oh rare Norgem, thou dost far exceed Beckley, Peasmarsh, Udimore and Brede.

A somewhat parochial comment!

OLD ROMNEY is just off the A259 coming from Rye on the way to New Romney. It was once a thriving port but now the sea is four miles away. It is said that the mound on which the church is built was the first island to appear as the sea receded from the Marsh. Today there is nothing much to see there except a sturdy little twelfth century building dedicated to St. Clement. In many ways I consider this to be the most memorable of the Marsh churches and a complete contrast to solitary Fairfield. Only a few houses are in the neighbourhood but St. Clement's is overshadowed by an enormous yew tree. There is no view of the sea and its situation is pleasantly rural. Inside, it is at once obvious that the church is loved and cared for. Fortunately for the visitor the Guide has been written by Anne Roper, an expert on Romney Marsh. Don't miss the remarkable font dating from 1300. Climb carefully into the Minstrels' Gallery and admire the big Royal Arms above the chancel arch, and good examples of the oval text boards, which are typical of the churches in this area. Notice also the worn oak steps leading up to the bell chamber. The box pews have been painted grey. John Piper claims that "The interior is one of the best and least spoiled Georgian interiors in the country, giving an excellent idea of what a village church was like a hundred and fifty years ago."

PETT. The village of this name stands high, a mile or more from the sea at the western end of Pett Level. It is not a show place but is in the heart of delightful country and within walking distance of Icklesham, Fairlight, the Fire Hills, and Guestling. And of course Winchelsea, either along the road behind the sea wall or down one of the most beautiful walks in the district known as Pannel Lane, past the windmill at Hog Hill. This narrow, winding lane is marked on the Ordnance Survey sheets 189 and 199. From Pett village it is an easy walk down Chick Hill to the sea at Cliff End where the marsh country finishes abruptly and the cliffs of Fairlight rise to the Fire Hills and terminate at Hastings Old Town. *[Ed. There are also two pubs in the village: The Royal Oak and The Two Sawyers. The latter has its own brewery and is a refreshing stop after a long walk.]*

PETT LEVEL is the stretch of reclaimed marsh between Winchelsea and the bluff known as Cliff End which also gives its name to the collection of bungalows and flats between the sea wall and the high ground on which the village of Pett stands a mile or more away. In the season Pett Level is busy and popular with holiday makers. Now it has a shop, a pub, a club and a little church. There is a bus service to Hastings through Fairlight.

Between the end of the sea wall and the cliff, the shingle bank has been greatly strengthened. This is a danger point at the time of very high tides, and on at least one occasion calamity was only just averted. Just inland, between the road and the line of old cliffs against which the sea once broke, is the end of the Royal Military Canal, built as a defence against Napoleon. It is nothing more than a reed-filled dyke here but it is three times as wide when it joins the Brede below Winchelsea, wider still when it joins the Rother at Rye and when it leaves the river at Iden Lock on the road to Appledore, it has become a noble, tree-lined canal, bounding the Marsh to the north and opening at Hythe.

The sea wall, which was built after the Second World War, is a fine defence against the hungry sea and runs beyond Winchelsea Beach. The Pett Level marsh is bounded on the north by a line of cliffs - along the top of which runs Pannel Lane, already mentioned under Pett - which eventually form the sandstone bluff on which Edward I built his New Winchelsea. This stretch of fertile marsh is of great interest to the naturalist and bird watcher. It was flooded during the last war because, as always, it was considered vulnerable from attack by sea. You may walk along the sea wall today although there is no longer any evidence of the underwater defences, only the remains of the wave screen built in the 1930s in front of the timber box-wall, standing like rows of blackened teeth along the beach. From this vantage point above the waves and the levels, you can also see two large meres close to the road. These stretches of water are usually busy with many varieties of birds. Indeed the wooded cliffs and lanes round Pett Level are a refuge for many migrants and, where the plough draws brown furrows across the Marsh, gulls squabble with rooks for the disturbed wire worms. Great white swans glide majestically over the still water of the dykes and the Royal Military Canal and, if you watch patiently, you may see the herons fishing.

RYE HARBOUR has an unfortunate approach and is nothing at all like its parent town. Nevertheless it is worth a visit and the road to take is off the A259 Winchelsea Road opposite Rye's Martello Tower to the south side of the town. It is clearly signposted (1½ miles) and almost immediately the road swings sharply left over the River Brede which has been wandering round Winchelsea and then, after being joined by the Royal Military Canal, turned north to Rye. There is some industrial development along the road to the village and nearby is the little Fishermen's Church. After a straggle of houses on each side, the road opens out and we realise that we are among boats hauled up on the mud, within reach of ships that may be going up or down to the sea, at the mouth of the Rother which is at least a mile away. Here is the Club House of the Rye Harbour Sailing Club, a ship's chandler's shop, two pubs and a small board listing the Lifeboats which served from here. The last name on the list is that of the *Mary Stanford*, the loss of which with every member of her crew, is described in Chapter Two. On the other side of the river are the sand dunes of Camber and the Club House of Rye's famous Golf Links. There is a big car park at Rye Harbour now, as well as a Caravan Camp, which is close to a very fine specimen of a Martello Tower surrounded by a dry moat. There is also a concrete road (cars forbidden) close to the west bank of the river, leading down to the river's mouth. To walk this at any time of the year is an invigorating experience and it is possible to extend your walk across the Marsh to Winchelsea Beach. There is a Nature Reserve on the western side and there are three hides to which the public has free access. It is worth taking binoculars because the views across the river to Dungeness to the east and, west across to Winchelsea and the Fairlight Hills beyond, are magnificent. The air is clean and bracing too.

SEDLESCOMBE is 11½ miles from Rye and not as far from Hastings just off the A21. From the former, the pleasanter way would be the B2089 along the Udimore ridge and through Broad Oak to Cripps Corner where you must turn sharp left on to the A229. Sedlescombe is usually described as a 'Show Village' as if it were unique in East Sussex! Nevertheless, it is very attractive because most of the houses, shops and pubs are set well back from the road with pleasant stretches of grass in front of them. There is a village pump on the Green, some thatched cottages and a bridge over the youthful River Brede.

SMALLHYTHE is little more than a hamlet on the road from Appledore to Tenterden not much more than seven miles from Rye. It is worth visiting in the summer months *[Ed. 1976]* to see the Ellen Terry Museum which is now a National Trust property and open most days during the season. The great Edwardian actress moved here from Tower Cottage in Winchelsea. It is difficult to appreciate that Smallhythe was once the port of Tenterden.

SNARGATE is another of the Marsh churches and is easily reached when you go to Fairfield. Turn south after leaving the latter and take the first lane on the left past Fairfield Court. The church of St. Dunstan's is opposite an inn a few yards off the B2080 from Appledore. The River Rother once flowed this way to New Romney and we are told that there was a sluice here to hold back the water. Richard Barham, author of *Ingoldsby Legends,* was appointed the parson of St. Dunstan's in 1817. The church is a sturdy, picturesque building with a tower leaning towards the Marsh and dwarfing some cottages built close to the churchyard. Even with passing traffic a few yards away it still seems incredible that it should ever have been built in such isolation. Not surprisingly this was one of the churches used by smugglers for hiding contraband. The interior has some good specimens of the Text Boards so often to be seen in the Marsh churches but somehow I have found it rather depressing.

STONE-IN-OXNEY should be seen for several reasons. Take the Appledore road from Rye and after crossing the Rother at Iden Lock - the Royal Military Canal is now on your right - you will notice a large bluff rising from the low lying Marsh in front of you. What you see is the Isle of Oxney and it is easy to imagine that the sea once lapped the cliffs which are now green hillsides. Just about here is the county boundary with Kent and soon after, turn left up a lane opposite a bridge across the canal. It is a sharp turn and the lane is narrow with several blind corners and it climbs steadily until you turn right at a signpost directing you to Stone Church which you can see ahead. This is a handsome fifteenth century building with a massive tower standing on a knoll above the road which about here is the highest part of the old cliffs. Before you go in, walk down the road a few yards and look over a field gate at the amazing view across the Marsh. Only from Lympne some miles further east where the escarpment is higher, is the prospect finer.

At first sight there is nothing special about the interior of St. Mary's church. Obviously it has been 'Victorianized' but the surprise stands on the floor of the belfry. My discovery of this block of stone is memorable because it gave me the idea for a story [Ed. Treasure at Amorys] which has pleased my readers ever since it was published in 1964. It is a Mithraic altar proving without doubt that it was left hereabouts by the armies of Rome when they landed on the Kentish coast. Mithras was the soldiers' god and it so happened that I had seen a similar altar carved with the Mithraic bull in St. Clement's, Rome which was built over a Mithraic temple. There are several stories as to how this one found its way into a Christian church but there seems agreement that it was dug out of a quarry or sandpit and used as a mounting block, either by the squire, or outside one of the inns. I like the suggestion that a parson recognized it and insisted that it should be placed in his church because Christianity conquered Mithraism. But it is still there and it is a sobering thought that it was carved in the third century. And close to this relic is something much older - the fossilized bones of a prehistoric dinosaur also dug out of a local quarry.

TENTERDEN is altogether delightful. A small, lively market town typical of the Kentish Weald with a broad main street bordered with beautiful greens in front of the shops. It is only ten miles from Rye on the B2082 through Playden, Iden, Wittersham (the biggest village on the Isle of Oxney) and Smallhythe. It is interesting that Tenterden was attached to Rye in 1449 as a member of the Cinque Ports Confederation. It was indeed an important gateway into Kent with Smallhythe as its port on the Rother. Ships were built here and it was once visited by Edward I, the monarch who planned New Winchelsea on its hill. I much admire the beautiful fronts of some of the wood and plaster houses on each side of the street. The parish church of St. Mildred (fifteenth century) has a magnificent pinnacled tower which is high enough for a beacon to be lit for shipping coming up the broad estuary to Smallhythe. You will see it on the skyline as you drive north long before you see Tenterden itself.

WINCHELSEA, although last in the alphabetical list of places worth visiting, should be first choice for any traveller lucky enough to find himself in Rye. The two 'Antient Towns' are only 2½ miles apart and their history is strongly linked. They are both Cinque Ports, they have both been deserted by the sea, they have both faced the same enemies and have suffered grievously from attacks by sea and by air and history proves that they have served Britain well. Both have been built on hills. Rye has no room to spare on her rocky pyramid. The Winchelsea we can explore today still gives an impression of space and grace. The streets are grass-verged and wide for a town which has under 500 inhabitants. Every road is at right angles to the next, exactly as planned in squares during the reign of Edward I, when the old town which had been built on a spit of shingle - probably off the sands of Camber - was finally engulfed by the sea in 1287. The hill on which the new town was built was known as Iham and there was a small village of that name on its western slopes. But Winchelsea is *not* a village and must never be referred to as such. It is a town and on Easter Monday 1975 when these words were written, Winchelsea, with becoming ceremony, elected its 681st Mayor.

Like Rye, its sister town, we are fortunate in our historians, particularly W. D. Cooper, who published his *History of Winchelsea* in 1850 *[Ed. And Malcolm Pratt who published his 'Winchelsea a Port of Stranded Pride' in 1998.]* The Official Guide, written by a previous Mayor, Captain H. Lovegrove, is extremely good. He tells briefly of Winchelsea's history and his suggestions of what to look for are admirable. There is also an excellent Guide on sale in the noble church dedicated to St. Thomas of Canterbury built in the very centre of the town. The great churchyard, is indeed, Winchelsea's only open space! *[Ed. Following the publication of Portrait of Rye in 1976 Malcolm Saville went on to write an updated Church Guide which is still on sale today. When Malcolm Saville died in 1982 his ashes were buried in the Garden of Remembrance at Winchelsea Church.]*

Winchelsea must be savoured slowly. Spring is perhaps best, when the churchyard is ringed with pink blossom. Early April is also unforgettable because then the newborn lambs are crying on the hillsides which were once dominated by the black skeleton of the old windmill. The latter was built in 1703 over the remains of a small church dedicated to St. Leonard but was destroyed by a storm in 1987. *[Ed.]* Winchelsea's Mill was a landmark for many miles. And in summer, when the roses bloom against the walls both white and grey, Winchelsea, the smallest *town* in England, welcomes many visitors. Golden autumn is superb when the sun sinks early over the Fire Hills on the western skyline. In winter, when the days are short and gales roar over the hill from the south-west, those of us who have made this 'Antient Town' our home have more time to remember, and be thankful for, the great king who planned our town with such care and that, like Rye, it has always helped to guard the shores of England and was not slow to fight for it.

Today, it is fashionable to refer to Winchelsea as if it were dead - or "dreaming on its hill" - but it is not true to say that it lives entirely in the past. It is still on the trunk road A259 and consequently great lorries still grind their way up Ferry Hill and shake the houses on the western side of the town.

Remember, please, when you wander along our grass-verged, wide street, that although this now peaceful little haven has seen bloodshed, pillage and piracy, the flags of the Cinque Ports, of St. George and the Union Flag itself are still hoisted over its ancient Court House and the church, on appropriate occasions.

Visit the church first. Then look across the Marsh to Camber Castle and the distant prospect of Dungeness from the Lookout in the shadow of the Strand Gate. Go to the green fields around the site of the old mill. Discover, if you can, the haunted ground of Deadman's Lane. Walk as far as the ruined New Gate down Pannel Lane where the French were treacherously admitted one Sunday morning in 1380. You will see here sections of the great ditch which was part of the town's defences.

Don't miss the splendid Museum in the Court Hall, or the ruins of Greyfriars in the grounds of the mansion of the same name. Or the Town Well in Castle Street.

The third gate into Winchelsea is called the Pipewell Gate. It is at the top of Ferry Hill. The ferry, of course, was across the Brede which, when the gate was built, was very wide and had to be crossed to reach Udimore on the ridge to the north.

There is much else to see. You cannot wander through these quiet streets without being conscious of the past because Winchelsea has somehow preserved the atmosphere of its beginnings. Writers and artists have been inspired by, and helped in, its preservation. There may be a brave new world waiting for us as we approach the twenty-first century but you will not see many signs of it in Winchelsea - the unforgettable and perfectly planned and beautiful little town on a hill.

WINCHELSEA BEACH, like Rye Harbour,. bears no resemblance to its parent town. A narrow road will take you there from the foot of Winchelsea town's Strand Hill. Eighty years ago this road, now bordered with bungalows, was a lane. Now it leads to a colony of holiday homes and caravan camps. Here are shops, a pub, a garage and a supermarket. Here too is Winchelsea's daughter church of St. Richard. At the church, keep left for a few hundred yards until you see the sea wall in front of you. Once, to the west of the Public Lavatories, was a row of coastguard cottages. There was no sea wall to protect them in those days - only a bank of shingle. Dog's Hill, now levelled for a small block of flats, was once crowned with a fisherman's hut and, half a mile or so along a rough road to Cliff End was the pub called "The Ship" which was washed away in the 1930s.

But if you would like an invigorating walk, leave the car, mount the sea wall and face east. Now you can see the mouth of the Rother, the gleam of Camber Sands and the great bulk of the Nuclear Power Station at Dungeness. Keep walking. The shacks and bungalows on your left are the homes of those who have found solace in this curious hinterland or those who come here in the summer months for sun and sea.

But walk on. The sea wall gives place to a bank of shingle and the road below is only for the use of the Authority responsible for keeping back the sea. But about here you will see a notice announcing the Rye Harbour Nature Reserve although you are asked not to walk across it to the Rother during the breeding and nesting season. A signposted footpath on a causeway above the Marsh takes you to an enormous mere of deep, dangerous water. Here there are sea birds in abundance. You can, if you wish, find your way across to the road leading from Rye Harbour to the mouth of the river.

This area of reclaimed land has a strange, haunting atmosphere. It is not beautiful. In winter it is lonely and windswept. The sands below the sea wall are popular in summer and there is plenty of shipping to watch in the Channel. Look west to Cliff End and the Fairlight Hills. Look back to the real Winchelsea and north-east to the line of cliffs below Iden and, even if Rye itself is difficult to see, you know now where it is, and has been, for a very long time.

RYE

It seems solid enough
As you come through the Landgate
And the streets climb up to the church
That, like a stranded ark,
Straddles the hilltop.

But Time is different here.
The streets are full of beggars
You cannot see, who speak
The tongues of centuries
To the deaf tourists,

'We have always been perverse
'And unprofessional beggars,
'For we want to give, not take,
'To offer you this town's
'Particular nature.

'It is not what you see
'As you trip on the cobbles
'And say the houses are quaint,
'Nor was it ever like that,
'It is our presence.

'The town keeps whispering
'Its history - fishermen, merchants –
'Lifetimes that have been built
'From unimportant scraps
'To construct a clement

'Enclave and sanctuary.
'Once you have understood this,
You will feel Rye within,
'And be disposed to come back,
'If you ever leave it.'

Patric Dickinson

Bibliography

A Guide to Romney Marsh by Ann Roper
   and the various Guides to individual Marsh Churches by the
   same author
A New History of Rye by Leopold Vidler (1934)
An Old Gate of England by A. G. Bradley (1917)
Highways and Byways in Sussex by E. V. Lucas (1923)
Kent Villages by Alan Bignell (1975)
Penguin Guide to Sussex by F. R. Banks
Romney Marsh by John Piper
Romney Marsh by Walter J. C. Murray (1956)
Rye Museum Publications
   including 'Old Inns and Ale Houses of Rye' by Geoffrey S.
   Bagley, 'Many A Bloody Affray', and 'Murder by Mistake'
   both by Kenneth M. Clark, and, by both these experts in
   collaboration, 'The Story of the Ypres Tower and Rye
   Museum'.
Rye Royal (Adams Illustrated Guide) by Jim Foster
Sussex by Esther Meynell
The Cinque Ports and Romney Marsh by Margaret Brentnall
The Cinque Ports by Ford Madox Hueffer (1900)
The Cinque Ports by R. and E. Jessup (1952)
The History of Winchelsea by W. D. Cooper (1850)
The Official Guide to Winchelsea by Captain H. Lovegrove
The Official Town Guide to Rye by Geoffrey S. Bagley
The Story of Lamb House, Rye by H. Montgomery Hyde (1966)
The Story of Two Ancient Towns by Ethel Macgeorge (1932)

Tudor Rye by Graham Hayhew (1987)
Winchelsea a Port of Stranded Pride by Malcolm Pratt (1998)

Appendix

Malcolm Saville:
Author of Publications for Children

KEY: 'xyz' Titles classed as fiction. "xyz" Titles classed as non-fiction.

- "Amateur Acting and Producing for Beginners"
    - D.J. Desmond (pseudonym); London, C. Arthur Pearson Ltd (1937)

1 'Mystery at Witchend',
    illustrated by G.E. Breary. London, Newnes (1943).
2 'Seven White Gates',
    illustrated by Bertram Prance. London, Newnes (1944).
3 "Country Scrap-Book for Boys and Girls",
    London, National Magazine Company (1944).
4 'The Gay Dolphin Adventure',
    illustrated by Bertram Prance. London, Newnes (1945).
5 'Trouble at Townsend',
    illustrated by Lunt Roberts. London, Transatlantic Arts (1945).
6 "Open Air Scrap-Book for Boys and Girls",
    London, Gramol (1945).
7 "Seaside Scrap-Book for Boys and Girls",
    London, Gramol (1946).
8 'Jane's Country Year',
    illustrated by Bernard Bowerman. London, Newnes (1946).
9 'The Secret of Grey Walls',
    illustrated by Bertram Prance. London, Newnes (1947).
10 'The Riddle of the Painted Box',
    illust. by Lunt Roberts. London, Transatlantic Arts (1947)
11 'Redshank's Warning',
    illustrated by Lunt Roberts. London, Lutterworth Press (1948).
12 'Two Fair Plaits',
    illustrated by Lunt Roberts. London, Lutterworth Press (1948).
13 'Lone Pine Five',
    illustrated by Bertram Prance. London, Newnes (1949).

14 'Strangers at Snowfell',
   illustrated by Wynne. London, Lutterworth Press (1949).
15 'The Master of Maryknoll',
   illustrated by Alice Bush. London, Evans (1950).
16 'The Sign of the Alpine Rose',
   illustrated by Wynne. London, Lutterworth Press (1950).
17 'The Flying Fish Adventure',
   illustrated by Lunt Roberts. London, Murray (1950).
18 "Adventure of the Life-Boat Service",
   London, Macdonald (1950).
19 'All Summer Through',
   illust. by Joan Kiddell-Monroe. London, Hodder & Stough. (1951)
20 'The Elusive Grasshopper',
   illustrated by Bertram Prance. London, Newnes (1951).
21 'The Buckinghams at Ravenswyke',
   illustrated by Alice Bush. London, Evans (1952).
22 'The Luck of Sallowby',
   illustrated by Tilden Reeves. London, Lutterworth Press (1952).
23 "Coronation Gift Book",
   London, Daily Graphic-Pitkins (1952).
24 'The Ambermere Treasure',
   illustrated by Marcia Lane Foster. London, Lutterworth (1953)
25 'Christmas at Nettleford',
   illust. by Joan Kiddell-Monroe.London, Hodder & Stough.(1953)
26 'The Secret of the Hidden Pool',
   illustrated by Lunt Roberts. London, Murray (1953).
27 'The Neglected Mountain',
   illustrated by Bertram Prance. London, Newnes (1953).
28 'Spring Comes to Nettleford',
   illustrated by Joan Kiddell-Monroe. London, Hod. & Stough. (1954).
29 'The Long Passage',
   illustrated by Alice Bush. London, Evans (1954).
30 'Susan, Bill and the Wolf Dog',
   illustrated by Ernest Shepard. London, Nelson (1954).
31 'Susan, Bill and the Ivy Clad Oak',
   illustrated by Ernest Shepard. London, Nelson (1954).
32 'Saucers over the Moor',
   illustrated by Bertram Prance. London, Newnes (1955).
   'Saucers over the Moon',
   Wendover, Bucks., Goodchild (1984).

33 'The Secret of Buzzard Scar',
   illustrated by Joan Kiddell-Monroe. London,Hod. & Stough. (1955)
34. 'Where the Bus Stopped',
   Oxford, Blackwell (1955).
35 'Susan, Bill and the Vanishing Boy',
   illustrated by Ernest Shepard. London, Nelson (1955).
36 'Susan, Bill and the Golden Clock',
   illustrated by Ernest Shepard. London, Nelson (1955).
37 'Susan, Bill and the Dark Stranger',
   illustrated by Ernest Shepard. London, Nelson (1956).
38 'Susan, Bill and the 'Saucy Kate',
   illustrated by Ernest Shepard. London, Nelson (1956).
39 'Young Johnnie Bimbo',
   illustrated by Lunt Roberts. London, Murray (1956).
40 'Wings Over Witchend',
   dustwrapper illustrated by Charles Wood. London, Newnes (1956).
41 'Lone Pine London',
   dustwrapper illustrated by Charles Wood. London, Newnes (1957).
42 'Treasure at the Mill',
   illustrated by Harry Pettit. London, Newnes (1957).
43 'The Fourth Key',
   illustrated by Lunt Roberts. London, Murray (1957).
44 'The Secret of the Gorge',
   dustwrapper illustrated by Charles Wood. London, Newnes (1958).
45 "King of Kings",
   London, Nelson (1958).
   "King of Kings",
   Berkhamsted, Herts., Lion (1975).
46 'Mystery Mine',
   dustwrapper illustrated by Terry Freeman. London, Newnes (1959).
47 'Four-and-Twenty Blackbirds',
   illustrated by Lilian Buchanan. London, Newnes (1959).
   'The Secret of Galleybird Pit',
   London, Armada (1967).
48 'Small Creatures' (Truth in a Tale Series),
   illustrated by John Kenney. London, Ward (1959).
49 'Sea Witch Comes Home',
   dustwrapper illustrated by Terry Freeman. London, Newnes (1960).
50 'Susan, Bill and the Bright Star Circus',
   illustrated by Terry Freeman. London, Nelson (1960).

51 'Susan, Bill and the Pirates Bold',
      illustrated by Terry Freeman. London, Nelson (1961).
52 "Malcolm Saville's Country Book",
      London, Cassell (1961).
53 'Not Scarlet But Gold',
      illustrated by A.R. Whitear. London, Newnes (1962).
54 "Malcolm Saville's Seaside Book",
      London, Cassell (1962).
55 'A Palace for the Buckinghams',
      illustrated by Alice Bush. London, Evans (1963).
56 'Three Towers in Tuscany',
      London, Heinemann (1963).
57 'The Purple Valley',
      London, Heinemann (1964).
58 'Treasure at Amorys',
      illustrated by Terry Freeman. London, Newnes (1964).
59 'Dark Danger',
      London, Heinemann (1965).
60 'White Fire',
      London, Heinemann (1966).
61 'The Thin Grey Man',
      illustrated by Desmond Knight. London, Macmillan (1966).
62 'Man With Three Fingers',
      illustrated by Michael Whittlesea. London, Newnes (1966).
63 'Strange Story',
      London, Mowbrays (1967).
64 "Come to London",
      London, Heinemann (1967).
65 'Power of Three',
      London, Heinemann (1968).
66 'Rye Royal',
      London, Collins (1969).
67 "Come to Devon",
      London, Benn (1969).
68 "Come to Cornwall",
      London, Benn (1969).
69 'Strangers at Witchend',
      London, Collins (1970).
70 'The Dagger and the Flame',
      London, Heinemann (1970).

71 "Come to Somerset",
   London, Benn (1970).
72 'Good Dog Dandy',
   London, Armada (1971).
73 'The Secret of the Villa Rosa',
   London, Collins (1971).
74 "See How It Grows",
   illust. by Robert Micklewright. London, Oxford Univ.Press (1971).
75 'Where's My Girl?',
   London, Collins (1972).
76 'The Roman Treasure Mystery',
   London, Armada (1973).
77 'Diamond in the Sky',
   London, Collins (1974).
78 "Eat What You Grow",
   illustrated by Robert Micklewright. London, Carousel (1975).
79 "Portrait of Rye",
   illustrated by Michael Renton. E. Grinstead, Sussex, Goulden (1976).
80 'Marston - Master Spy',
   London, Heinemann (1978).
81 'Home to Witchend',
   London, Armada (1978).
82 "The Countryside Quiz",
   illustrated by Robert Micklewright. London, Carousel (1978).
83 "Wonder Why Book of Exploring a Wood",
   illustrated by Elsie Wrigley.London,Transworld (1978).
84 "Wonder Why Book of Exploring the Seashore",
   illustrated by Jenny Heath. London, Trans.(1979).
85 "Words for All Seasons",
   illust. by Elsie & Paul Wrigley.Guildford, Surrey, Lutterworth (1979).
86 "Wonder Why Book of Wild Flowers Through the Year",
   illustrated by Elsie Wrigley. London, Transworld (1980).
87 "The Seashore Quiz",
   illustrated by Robert Micklewright. London, Carousel (1981).
88 "The Story of Winchelsea Church",
   Sussex, Winchelsea Church. (circa. 1980).
89 "The Silent Hills of Shropshire",
   illustrated by John Allsup. Worcester, O'Hanlon (1998).

Index

Appledore 90-91, 99, 110

Bagley, Geoffrey 15, 60-61, 77
Battle 82, 91-92
Benson, E.F. 38, 43, 78
Bodiam 92-93
Borough Arms, The 74
Breads, John 28-30, 50, 51, 81
Brede 93-94
Brede, River 10, 54, 55, 56, 67-68, 72-73, 83
Brookland 94-95, 99, 103

Camber 95-96, 104
Camber Castle 10, 13, 20, 40, 54, 68, 89, 96-97, 114
Camber Sands 16, 47, 55, 56, 89, 96, 109, 113, 115
Church Square, Rye 12, 30, 38, 51, 53, 63, 64, 78-80
Cinque Ports Hotel 34
Cinque Ports Street, Rye 12, 59, 84, 85
Clark, Kenneth 15, 31
Cliff End 56, 101, 107, 115, 116
Confederation of the Cinque Ports 16, 18, 20

Dungeness 11, 33, 39-40, 47, 48, 90, 91, 97-98, 101, 109, 114, 115

Eastcliff, Rye 13, 47
East Street, Rye 21, 48, 49, 50, 54, 76, 86
Elders House 25, 74
Elizabeth I 13, 20, 21-22, 54, 105

Fairfield 98-100, 103
Fairlight 56, 68, 69, 70, 87, 100-101, 107, 109, 116
Fletcher's House 40, 61-63
Flushing Inn 12, 28, 49-50, 87
Friars of the Sack 64

George I 25-26
George Hotel, The 61
Godden, Rumer 42
Grebell, Allen 25, 26-30, 43, 81
Grebell, Thomas 25
Griz Nez 47
Guestling 70
Gungarden, The 11, 14, 51, 54, 55, 68, 86, 87

Hartshorn House 23, 74
Hastings 10, 16, 18, 31, 33, 35, 60, 68-69, 89, 90, 91-92, 97, 101-102
Hawkhurst Gang 32, 76
Henry III 16
Henry VIII 20, 40, 89, 97
Heritage Centre 30, 51, 73, 81

High Street, Rye 11, 12, 22, 26, 48-49, 59, 60, 87
Hilders Cliff 47, 56, 57, 58
Holloway, William 15, 18-19, 42
Hope Anchor Inn 37, 67, 68, 74, 81, 87
Huguenot Refugees 9, 20-21, 22, 24, 46, 49, 86
Hythe 10, 31, 89, 101

Icklesham 70
Isle of Oxney 91, 111-112
Ivychurch 103, 105

James, Henry 42, 78
Jeake, Samuel (I-III) 15, 23, 24-25, 40, 74
Jeakes' House / Storehouse 24-25, 42, 74-76

La Rochelle, Rye 21, 49, 50
Lamb House 25, 26, 28, 33, 38, 42, 76, 78, 81
Lamb, James 25-30, 43, 78
Lamb, Thomas 32-33
Landgate, The 12, 25, 46
Lion Street, Rye 10, 12, 22, 40, 61-63, 80
Lucas, E.V. 71, 92, 106
Lydd 48, 90, 91, 103-104

Market Street, Rye 12, 49, 50, 51, 61, 63-64, 80, 86
Martello Bookshop, The 60
Mary Stanford (Lifeboat) 36-37, 109

Mermaid Inn, The 32, 67, 76-78, 85, 87
Mermaid Street, Rye 12, 23, 25, 42, 64, 67, 68, 73-78, 80, 81, 82
Mint, The (Rye) 11, 12, 30, 77, 84-85, 86, 87
Monastery Restaurant 48, 59

New Romney 18, 91, 98, 104-105, 106, 110
Northiam 21, 105-106

Old Grammar School 22-23, 60-61
Old Romney 90, 106
Owlers, The 31

Peacocke, Thomas 22-23, 60-61
Pett 11, 70, 71, 90, 107
Pett Level 10, 39, 56, 100, 107-108
Pump Street, Rye 12, 51-53

Quaker House 25, 74

Romney, Hythe & Dymchurch Railway 97, 105
Romney Marsh 10, 14, 31, 94, 106
Rope Walk, Rye 12, 59
Roper, Anne 94-95, 106
Rother, River 10, 11, 13, 18, 35, 47, 55, 56, 91, 102, 110
Royal Military Canal 10, 89, 91, 101, 107-108, 109, 111

Rye Art Gallery 48, 49
Rye Harbour 11, 34, 35, 36-37, 39, 54, 72, 96, 108-109, 115, 116
Rye Lodge Hotel 47

St. Anthony's 63
St. Anthony of Padua Church 66, 72
St. Leonard's-on-Sea 101
St. Mary the Virgin Church 10, 11, 14, 18, 19, 20, 24, 25, 26, 28, 40, 61, 72, 80-81
St. Thomas of Canterbury Church (Winchelsea) 113
Saville, Reverend A.T. 32, 43, 58-59
Sedlescombe 109
Ship Inn, The 38, 67, 86, 87
Smallhythe 110, 112
Snargate 110
Standard Inn, The 85
Stone-in-Oxney 110-111
Strandgate 25, 30, 67, 73, 85, 86
Strand House 38

Tenterden 112
Tillingham, River 54, 55, 56, 67, 72-73, 83, 84, 87
Tower House 47, 57-58

Tower Street, Rye 12, 57
Town Hall 12, 30, 50-51, 64, 77
Town Salts, Rye 13, 33, 34, 47, 48, 54, 56, 86
Trader's Passage 12, 38, 42, 68, 74, 81-82, 86, 87
Turkey Cock Lane 46, 57, 58

Union Inn, The 49, 50

Vidler, Leopold Amon 15, 16, 21, 24, 25-26, 34, 36, 42, 43, 53-54, 57, 67

Watchbell Street, Rye 12, 53, 64, 66-68, 72, 81-82, 86, 87
West Street, Rye 25, 33, 38, 78
Winchelsea 9, 10, 13, 15, 16, 18, 19, 20, 36, 39, 54, 68, 71-72, 80, 89, 95, 100, 102, 107, 108, 110, 112-115, 116
Winchelsea Beach 72, 100, 109, 115-116
Wish Street, Rye 12, 85
Wish Ward, Rye 12, 85, 86

Ye Olde Tucke Shoppe 50
Ypres Castle Inn 86
Ypres Tower 12, 18, 30, 38, 40, 49, 51, 53-54, 55, 87

Have you read the companion volume to
Portrait of Rye?

Available from all good bookshops or direct from
the Publisher for £8.99 (ISBN 0 9528059 1 X) at:

10 Bilford Road, Worcester WR3 8QA.

[Please make cheques payable to Mark O'Hanlon.
Orders despatched within 28 days – UK postage paid]

The Malcolm Saville Society
10 Bilford Road, Worcester WR3 8QA

The Malcolm Saville Society was formed in 1994 to bring together fans of Malcolm Saville's work.

Through regular magazines and meetings, the Society allows enthusiasts to exchange news, information and speculation about the books and the locations that inspired them.

Now in its sixth year, the Society has enrolled over 450 people of all ages and continues to welcome new members. It is currently preparing to celebrate the centenary of Malcolm Saville's birth in 2001.

For further details please send a SAE to the above address.